the (creative)

College
Guide

the game of find/apply/decide

Sallie Ough Nangeroni

ISBN: 1463601654
ISBN-13: 9781463601652

to Dena & Fiona
my creative & magnificently fun students

to James, Charlie & Ben
my creative & constantly amazing sons

and to Jim Dear
my creative & brilliant traveling scientist

the (creative) **College Guide**
the game of find/apply/decide

You're smart, right?

Sometimes being considered smart is great. Learning is usually easy for you, in and out of school. You have curiosity about the world and lots of interests and talents. You might be good at debating relevant issues with your peers in the classroom, or enjoy sharing inspired, amusing ideas with your friends in the cafeteria.

Sometimes being smart isn't so great. It can mean higher expectations of success from others. You might be a perfectionist: you don't want to disappoint anyone by making mistakes. Or you may be a procrastinator: you honestly believe a task will get done eventually, so why the rush? You might be an under-achiever: the pressure to do your best makes it easier to do very little or nothing at all. If you don't do anything, you can't disappoint anyone, including yourself.

When it comes to college, being smart can mean that many people assume that you'll be accepted at any school, anywhere. Unfortunately college applications don't use IQ scores as criteria for admission. Just being "smart" won't cut it. What can you do to find a college you want, that also wants you?

the (creative) *College Guide* isn't about standardized testing, applications, scholarships, finances, getting recommendations, or your history of community service. It doesn't rank colleges, refer you to specific schools in specific locations, or recommend schools. *the Guide* is a thinking book, a question book, a book about you, about colleges, and your life in the next few years.

- What if finding out more about yourself can help you find colleges that fit your interests, abilities, and learning styles?

- What if creative thinking can help you play with ideas, think on the side, under, or above the box, and consider options to a number of schools?

- What if understanding the basics of business can show you how college visibility, appeal, and admissions work?

- What if taking intelligent risks and following through with your creative ideas help you discover, explore, and possibly apply to colleges you'd hadn't even considered?

- What if you're accepted, rejected, or something in between?

You can be successful in the crazy college game, but you can't win if you don't play.

Intelligence + Imagination = Success

You're smart, right?
Let's play!

....

Whether you believe you can,
or whether you believe you can't,
you're absolutely right.

Henry Ford (1863-1947) founder of the Ford Motor Company

....

How to Use the Guide

Maybe your parents bought this book for you. Maybe you bought it for yourself. Maybe you got it as a present. Maybe you bought it for a class. Wherever you got it, this is your book.

Read this book all at once. Read it by chapters. Read it in pieces. Read it backward, from the last chapter to the first. Read it during study hall, on a family trip in the car, in your room, in the bathroom.

Be neat. Use a bookmark. Write down questions, observations, and opinions. Stick on sticky notes. Underline relevant sentences and words, circle comments or ideas you disagree with, circle ideas and comments you like.

Be messy. Fold down the pages where you stopped reading or where you find something interesting. Use a highlighter, or six highlighters in different colors. Use a pen, a pencil, crayons, and/or markers. Make charts, doodle, illustrate. Draw arrows between ideas that connect. Write in the margins.

Talk to yourself in your head or out loud about information, thinking, imagining.
Ask other people what they know, think, imagine.
Tell your dog, cat, or iguana what you know, think, and imagine.

Interact with your book. Have fun with your book.
Use your book in ways you learn best.

NOTE: If you borrowed this book from a friend (who said to please return it) or your school bought it for classes (to return at the end of the semester), you probably shouldn't mark it up. Taking notes on a separate piece of paper isn't the only answer.

What if you could do whatever you do to do it and do it well?

Chapter 1
Personality & Learning Styles

Who do you think you are?
(and what if you're not?)

....

What you think of yourself is much more important
than what others think of you.

Seneca (45 BC–65 AD) Roman philosopher

....

How many times have you heard people say, "just be yourself?" What does that mean anyway? It seems we're always labeled by our age, sex, race, financial status, religious beliefs, sexual orientation, political position, weight, clothes, haircut, hair color, where we live, who we hang out with, the music we listen to, the books and movies we like, the video games we play, where we go to high school, our grades, our standardized test scores, and where we want to go to college. Can one label accurately describe you? What if you dress emo, but have a GPA of 4.0 and volunteer at a homeless shelter on weekends? What if you're the school comedian, hate school, but get perfect scores on standardized tests? What if you're the star soccer player who plays in a garage band and plans a career in pediatrics?

"Who am I?" is life's cosmic question. Throughout history, cultures created their own ways to classify and understand people: Egyptian astrology, French handwriting analysis, the Chinese zodiac, Greek numerology. Modern psychologists have developed testing techniques to discover how you think and how you learn. Are you an introvert in social situations? An analytical thinker in class? A doodler when you take notes? Can personality analysis or learning strengths give you insight into your identity?

So who do you think you are anyway?

Take a look at three personality and learning style models and see if you recognize yourself. You may be surprised. Or not.

It all depends on who you are.

....

Here's some simple advice: Always be yourself.
Never take yourself too seriously.
And beware of advice from experts, pigs,
and members of Parliament.

Kermit the Frog (1955-) Muppet

....

An Absolutely Bare-Bones Crash Course in…
Left-Brain/Right Brain Theory

Left-Brain/Right-Brain identification recognizes how you see the world and solve problems. Do you use Logic (left) or Intuition (right)?

Left-Brained is *The Analytical Thinker*
Uses a linear and logical process of learning

Famous Left-Brainers:

Friedrich Miescher (1844-1895) physician who discovered DNA

Thomas Edison (1847-1931) inventor

Marie Curie (1867-1934) physician & chemist

Steven Hawking (1942-) theoretical physicist

Bill Gates (1955-) computer magnate

When is this due?
Should I use a pen or a pencil?
Is this going to be in the test?
Can I have more time?
Did I do this right?

- -

Be less curious about people and more curious about ideas.

Marie Curie (1867-1934) physician & chemist

- -

Right-Brained is *The Global Thinker*
Uses flexible and intuitive reasoning to learn

Famous Right-Brainers:

Leonardo de Vinci (1452–1519) inventor & artist

William Shakespeare (1564-1616) poet & playwright

Wolfgang Mozart (1756–1791) musician & composer

Mary Cassatt (1844–1926) Impressionist painter

Albert Einstein (1879-1955) mathematician

Can I do it later?
Why are we doing this?
I can't work when it's quiet.
Can I do it a different way?
I need a break.

....

I am enough of an artist to draw freely upon
my imagination. Imagination is more important
than knowledge. Knowledge is limited.
Imagination encircles the world.

Albert Einstein (1879-1955) mathematician

....

What does Left-Brain/Right-Brain have to do with college?

In the 1960's, neurobiologist Dr. Roger Sperry analyzed results of surgery used to prevent seizures in severely epileptic patients. Sperry discovered that after cutting the nerve connectors between the two sides of the brain, a patient responded differently when presented with the same stimulus. For example, the right side of the patient's brain knew the name of an object, but couldn't explain what it was used for. The patient's left side could demonstrate the object's use, but couldn't name it. One side of the brain couldn't communicate with the other. Dr. Sperry concluded that the right side of the brain operates regions of visual, spatial, perceptual, and intuitive information, while the left side manages logic, verbal communication, numbers, and analytical thinking. Dr. Sperry was awarded the Nobel Prize in Medicine in 1981 for his research.

Via brain scanning and computer analysis, today's technology has shown that Sperry was right: the two hemispheres of the brain have to work together to fully communicate. For instance, while the left side controls your grammar and word choice, the right side controls your tone of voice and emphasis when you speak. The words "You're so smart." (left side) can be interpreted in different ways depending on how you say it (right side): "You're so smart!" "You're soooo smart." "You're so *smart*?" When you text, use online networks, or email (left) you can't use vocal inflection (right), so the meaning of your words may be misconstrued. Emoticons help: "You're so smart :D" "You're so smart :P" " You're so smart X(." We may favor one side of the brain, but we couldn't function without the other.

How can your right- or left-brain strengths influence your college choices?

Everyone has an inborn preference for using one side of the brain or the other: Intuition (right) or Logic (left). This inclination influences our thinking mode and our behavior. If you're an intuitive right-brained person you might consider a school's aesthetics and energy: the campus tour, dormitories, the "feel" of the campus, cultural diversity, or the variety of academic and extracurricular opportunities. If you're an analytical left-brained person you might focus on the facts and figures: the number of students, academic departments, credentials of instructors and professors, financing, schedules, or required credit hours.

If you're a preferred left-brainer and find yourself looking at a school by the numbers, take a break, turn right, and look around to get a feel for the place, too. If your brain leans to the right, make a logical left turn and get the facts.

Right or left, be conscious of how your brain works and learn to work both sides to collect information, explore possibilities, and make sound decisions about colleges.

• •

The great pleasure and feeling in my right-brain is more than my left-brain can find the words to tell you.

Roger Sperry (1913-1994) neurobiologist & neuropsychologist

• •

An Absolutely Bare-Bones Crash Course in...
The Myers-Briggs Type Indicator (MBTI)

Understanding your personality type improves your ability to communicate with other people. The Myers-Briggs Type Indicator assesses how you interact with others, how you learn, how you make decisions, and how you see the world. The inventory identifies sixteen possible personality types, based on responses to a series of statements in four areas. Your results are an acronym, e.g. ESTJ (Extrovert Sensing Thinking Judging).

How do you focus attention and create energy?

> Extroversion (E): from people and activity
> Introversion (I): from ideas and experiences

How do you take in information?

> Sensing (S): focused on the real and concrete
> Intuition (N): focused on patterns and meanings

How do you make decisions?

> Thinking (T): through logical analysis
> Feeling (F): with concern for your impact on others

How do you look at and approach the world?

> Judging (J): in a planned orderly way
> Perceiving (P): with flexibility and spontaneity

For many people, MBTI results aren't static. You could be assessed as an Extrovert on a day when you're looking forward to a party, or an Introvert on a day when you're studying hard for a test. Sometimes you may score in the middle, as both an Introvert and an Extrovert. But your overall responses on the MBTI can help you recognize who you are, how you think, and how you approach a problem.

Many businesses use this instrument as team training for employees. The MBIT can reveal employee strengths for team success: Who's good with people? Who likes to organize? Who is concerned with how this project will impact others?

Isabel Briggs Myers and her mother, Katharine Cook Briggs, created the MBTI inventory during World War II, based on psychiatrist C. G. Jung's theory of psychological types. Myers and Briggs believed that all people should understand and appreciate human differences. Myers continued her research and development of this inventory until she died in 1980. The MBTI is the most widely used tool in the world for defining personality type.

••

I dream that long after I'm gone,
my work will go on helping people.

Isabel Briggs Myers (1897-1980) psychological theorist

••

What does the Myers-Briggs Type Indicator have to do with college?

Select *Yes* or *No* to the statements that best describe you.

> 1) I enjoy solitary walks.
> 2) I like socializing with a group of people.
> 3) I usually speak softly.
> 4) I like to sit in the back of a classroom.

Based on your responses, the number of *Yes*'s and *No*'s describe you. For example, if you said *Yes* to 1, 3, and 4, and *No* to 2, you'd score as an Introvert. The real MBTI obviously has many more questions than this example, for all eight personality traits.

Understanding your personality type can help you ask questions that reflect what's immediately important to you, and recognize important questions that you hadn't thought of before.

What if I'm an Introvert (I)?
> *Should I even consider a big college?*

What if I'm an Extrovert (E)?
> *Would I get to meet different kinds of people at a small school?*

What if I use my Senses (S) to gather information?
> *Can I get from my dorm to class to the cafeteria to the fitness center easily?*

What I'm Intuitive (N) about seeing the meaning of information?
> *Do the kids on campus look happy?*

What if I Think (T) to make decisions?
> *What kind of financial aid and scholarships do they have?*

What if Feel (F) to weigh choices?
> *If a school is far away, can my parents afford to fly me home for breaks?*

What if I Judge (J) concrete factors?
> *Which schools have more opportunities for internships or study abroad?*

What if I Perceive (P) possibilities?
> *What if we could visit all the schools I like in one trip?*

Once you recognize your preferred personality traits, it's easier to try another one on. If your results of the MBIT assess you as a *Judge* who's collecting facts, pretend you're also a *Perceiver*, checking out the lifestyle of a school. Your balanced thinking will help you see and discover the unique qualities and opportunities of a college, and of yourself.

An Absolutely Bare-Bones Crash Course in...
Howard Gardner's Multiple Intelligences

Choose the categories below that reflect who you are as a learner:

Verbal/Linguistic: talker, reader, writer, word-player, poet

Logical/Mathematical: math whiz, fact-organizer, computer fan

Visual/Spatial: creator, artist, map-reader, doodler

Bodily/Kinesthetic: sports-person, jiggler, active mover and shaker

Musical/Rhythmic: singer, instrumentalist, rhymer, song-remember-er

Interpersonal: leader, people organizer, team player

Intrapersonal: independent, individualist, diary-writer, deep thinker

Naturalist: woods-walker, nature-watcher, observer, classifier

How many categories did you choose? Actually, every person is a combination of all eight intelligences, some stronger than others. Like the MBIT, Multiple Intelligences are measured by a *Yes/No* inventory, like "I enjoy playing baseball." (Kinesthetic), "My mood changes when I listen to music." (Musical), or "I can recognize and name the birds in my yard." (Naturalist). Knowing your strengths and building on your weaknesses, you can make better choices and decisions.

Developmental psychologist and professor of Cognition and Education at Harvard, Dr. Howard Gardner developed the theory of Multiple Intelligences in 1983. He believes that intelligence can't be measured by IQ or standardized tests, but by the ability to solve problems and create new ideas. Gardner works with teachers and educators across the country teaching how to identify apply and develop all eight intelligences in their schools and classrooms.

. . . .

If I were facing a career decision today, I think it unlikely that I would elect to go into psychology. Instead, I would search for the current career options that allow me maximum latitude to pursue my interests in human nature, systematic understanding, and communication with others. And that is precisely the advice I give to young persons who seem dead set on a certain career: "Don't choose the career first; decide what you want to do, and then see which careers are most likely to allow you maximum opportunities and flexibility in
the decades ahead."

Howard Gardner (1943-) psychologist & educator

. . . .

What do Multiple Intelligences have to do with college?

The original model of learning style identifies learners by one of four strengths: *Auditory* (learn by listening and discussing), *Visual* (learn by seeing and watching), *Tactile* (learn by recording ideas and hands-on activity), or *Kinesthetic* (learn by moving and doing). You automatically use your strongest style to see the world and approach problems. Being aware of and developing your three weaker areas can provide you with different ways to learn and problem-solve.

Howard Gardner expanded the list from four learning styles to eight. He believes that everyone has all eight intelligences, whether they know it or not. For example: one person enjoys giving painting classes for kids. Another person plays with a local band. These two people define themselves as an artist (Visual) and a musician (Auditory). The spin is that that artist may not realize that he uses geometry when creating a painting's composition (Mathematics) and plans hikes in the mountains based on what he hopes to discover on the trail (Kinesthetic and Naturalist). The musician uses spatial skills and logic to figure out how many people will fit in her apartment when she's having a party for her band (Visual and Mathematics) and prefers to be alone while writing lyrics (Intrapersonal).

Sometimes we're content with doing only what we do well. Gardner believes that that mind-set limits your personal growth. Recognizing who we are, we build on our strengths: "I'm great playing rugby. I think I'll practice with the older players more this season so I can move to a higher level team next year." Finding and developing our weaker skills, we can become more balanced, with broader interests and new ways to learn: "I'm not great in science, but I do love nature. Maybe I'll take Environmental Biology next semester for my science requirement."

When choosing colleges, consider schools that will encourage your obvious and acknowledged abilities, but also give you the chance to try something new and learn in different ways. You're not the same person now that you were as a high school freshman. Your interests have changed a lot over the last few years. Who will you be when you graduate from college? This is the perfect time to branch out and develop all eight of your multiple intelligences.

Your Personality & Learning Style...

Based on what you're learned in this chapter, what five words would best describe your personality and learning style?

Ask a close friend to describe your personality and your learning style in five words.

Ask your parent, teacher, or other adult to describe your personality and learning style in five words.

Ask someone in a class or your homeroom who you don't know well to describe your personality and your learning style in five words. (Tell him or her that this is homework.)

Are the words these people chose to describe your personality similar to the words you used?

Are the words these people used to describe your learning style similar to the words you used?

Did anyone say something about your personality or your learning style that surprised you?

Each chapter in the Guide *closes with a topical Twiz about successful people, where they went to college, and their undergraduate majors. Do the schools they attended surprise you? Do the majors they chose then relate to their careers now?*

Twizes are in different formats for different learners: some difficult, some easy. Here's an easy one. BTW, answers are not upside down at the end of each twiz because you can probably read upside down. (Please see the last page of the Guide *for answers.)*

The Celebrity Twiz

Actors assume different personalities in their work.
Match these performers to their entertainment resumes.

a) Adam Sandler
b) John Krasinski
c) Jon Stewart
d) Samuel L. Jackson
e) Natalie Portman
f) Matthew McConaughey
g) Tina Fey
h) Jane Lynch
i) Will Ferrell
j) Maggie Gyllenhaal

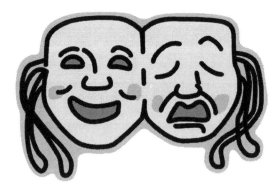

1) Got a degree in English from Columbia University (NY). Starred in *The Dark Night* and *Crazy Heart,* and has a brother who's also in the business.

2) Went to the University of Virginia studying Drama. Started out on *Saturday Night Live*, then broke into writing, producing, directing, and starring in a hit *SNL* parody on TV.

3) Graduated from New York University, majoring in Fine Arts. Wrote, produced, directed, and starred in block-buster comedy movies including *You Don't Mess with the Zohan, The Water Boy,* and *Big Daddy.*

4) Attended Morehouse College (GA), majoring in Drama. Best known for comic action roles in *Pulp Fiction, Snakes on a Plane,* and *Inglourious Basterds.*

5) Went to Harvard University (MA) for a degree in Psychology. Starred in the *Star Wars* trilogy while in college and won an Oscar for a film about a troubled dancer.

6) Attended the University of Texas–Austin, majoring in Film. Popular for both comedy roles in movies, including *How to Lose a Guy in 10 Days*, *Tropic Thunder*, and dramatic roles like *The Lincoln Lawyer*.

7) Graduated from University of Southern California (USC) studying Sports Information. Started out on *Saturday Night Live*, then moved on to comic movies including *Anchorman*, *Old School*, and *Elf*.

8) Went to the Illinois State University for a degree in Theater. Best known for films like *Best in Show* and *The Forty-Year-Old Virgin*, now happily famous for starring in *Glee* on TV.

9) Graduated from Brown University (RI) with a degree in Theater Arts. Starred in the film *Away We Go*, but still works the weekly comic grind as a salesperson for a TV paper company.

10) Earned a degree in Psychology from the College of William and Mary (VA). Entertains and informs cable TV millions with sharp comedy and political irony four nights a week.

(Personal Space. Who are you anyway?)

Chapter 2
Creative Thinking

What if your new (and expensive) cell phone fell into a fish tank full of expensive (and hungry) piranhas?

....

"Why, sometimes I've believed as many as six impossible things before breakfast."

Lewis Carroll (1832-1898) author
The White Queen, from Through the Looking Glass (1871)

....

Open the junk drawer in your kitchen, pull out all the writing instruments you can find, and set them on the table. How many pens, pencils, highlighters, colored pencils, crayons, and/or markers did you find? Sort them by type: all pens, all pencils, etc. Which do you like most? Which don't you like? Separate them by size, color, practicality, function. Are they constructed the same way? Plastic? Metal? Wax? Do they operate in different ways? They all write, but what else could you do with them? If you wanted to use them in an unusual way, what could you add? What would you take away? Are there any other ways of writing that are in the same drawer? Are there other ways of writing that aren't in this drawer? Where would you find them? How would you use them?

Sorting through your drawer, thinking about what you see, and looking at the process of writing in different ways, you may have just invented a newer, faster way for the technical world to communicate. You may have designed a new, undetectable way to doodle during class. You may have created a new, groundbreaking way to perform microsurgery. Great ideas are anywhere. Give

ideas a chance to emerge from the junk drawer of your amazing, malleable, creative brain. They're there.

It doesn't matter if you want to be an artist, a dentist, or a chemical engineer, creativity is a tool you'll use for life. In this chapter you'll explore three creativity models: one technical assessment of an individual's creativity, one a playful look at how we look when we look (if we look), and one a free-form map of your mind.

Think, open your mind, fiddle with possibilities, then decide.
This is the creative process.

· ·

The real innovation and creativity always comes from people crossing borders, crossing boundaries, thinking differently and very often through the interaction of disciplines through applying ideas from one field into another field. The real vitality of intelligence and creative thinking is in making connections, not from keeping everything separate.

Sir Ken Robinson (1950-) author & leader in creative innovation

· ·

For Your Consideration, a Condensed Consultation on…

The Torrance Test of Creative Thinking (TTCT)

The Torrance Test of Creative Thinking takes the test-taker through a series of verbal (e.g. "What happened when the cow jumped over the moon?") and non-verbal (e.g. "Create a picture using a triangle and lines.") exercises. Scores indicate the test-taker's creative abilities based these four behaviors:

Fluency: coming up with lots and lots and lots and lots of ideas

Flexibility: creating and exploring variations in ideas

Originality: creating distinctive ideas that are new and unusual

Elaboration: adding to and expanding on ideas

Figural TTCT, *Thinking Creatively with Pictures*, has three sections of picture-related exercises. This instrument looks for creative strengths like visualization, emotion, sense of humor, and thinking "outside the box." This thirty-minute test is for Kindergarteners to adults.

The verbal section of the TTCT, *Thinking Creatively with Words*, has six parts assessing the test-taker's creative skills of questioning, imagining possibilities, and improving ideas. It's designed for first graders to adults and takes forty-five minutes.

E. Paul Torrance was a professor of Educational Psychology at the University of Georgia and one of the first researchers of creativity. He believed that an IQ test was an incomplete assessment of intelligence. Torrance developed the TTCT to assess creative abilities of both children and adults. Scores on the TTCT are based on age and/or grade level. Because there are no "wrong" answers on the test, it can be administered more than once. Through innovative programs and his many published writings in books and journals, Torrance's work has encouraged the understanding and recognition of creativity's importance in schools and in the workplace.

Creative thinking is the process of sensing difficulties, problems, gaps in information, missing elements, something askew; making guesses and hypotheses about the solution of these deficiencies; evaluating and testing these hypotheses; possibly revising and restating them; and finally communicating the result.

E. Paul Torrance (1915-2003) educator & researcher

What does the TTCT have to do with college?

Follow Torrance's four components of creative thinking during your college search.

Fluency
Are you fluent in language? People who are fluent don't have to think about syntax before speaking. They already know the words.

Are you fluent in colleges? Are you finding and looking at many colleges, not just one or two? Are you exploring without immediate judgment?

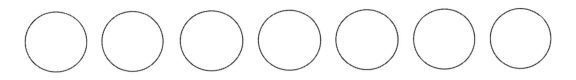

....

The best way to get an idea is to get a lot of ideas.

Linus Pauling (1901-1994) scientist & two-time Nobel Prize winner

....

Flexibility
Are you physically flexible? Can you bend, twist, kneel, jump, smile, or frown?

Are you mentally flexible when thinking about colleges? Are you willing to explore possibilities? Are you willing to change your mind?

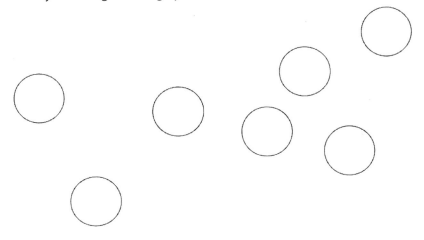

The idea for any cartoon (my experience, anyway)
is rarely spontaneous. Good ideas usually evolve
out of pretty lame ones, and vice versa.

Gary Larson (1950-) cartoonist: The Far Side

Originality

Are you an original thinker? Are you a musician, an artist, a comedian, a writer, an inventor?

Are you only looking at colleges that you've heard about or where a relative went or where your friends want to go? Would you explore schools that are new to you? Would you look for novel opportunities in a college?

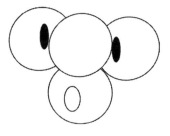

Every really new idea looks crazy at first.

Alfred North Whitehead (1861-1947) mathematician & philosopher

Elaboration

Do you elaborate by paying attention to the details? Do you insert descriptors in your writing, texture to your paintings, an unexpected twist to a presentation or experiment?

Are you looking at the details of a college? What criteria could you add to your search that would expand your knowledge about a school?

It's kind of fun to do the impossible.

Walt Disney (1901-1966) animator & filmmaker

Whether you're looking for colleges, creating an idea for an application, or making a decision about where to apply, keep an open mind. As Torrance himself would advise, be fluent in finding your options, flexible in your thinking, original in your perspective, and elaborate on your new ideas.

There are many ways of doing something.
Look for what no one has done before.

Jim Henson (1936 – 1990) creator of the Muppets

For Your Consideration, a Condensed Consultation on...
von Oech's Four Roles of the Creative Process

Remember that second grade teacher who sweetly said, "Now, put on your thinking caps!"? In this model, the creative thinker has four thinking caps and uses them all. The Explorer has a bug-free jungle pith helmet. The Artist wears a wildly unique beret. The Judge dons a stylish curly white wig, and The Warrior sports a dazzling horned Viking helmet. How can playing with these four characters hone your creativity skills?

Explorer: *What are you looking for?*

Search for and gather lots and lots and lots and lots of ideas and information in lots and lots of unexpected places (or right in front of your nose).

Artist: *Play with all of the ideas you found.*

Think outside and on the sides and in the bottom of the box. (And what's wrong with looking inside the box, too?) Go where there's no right or wrong. Mix information up. See what fits. Laugh!

Judge: *What's right? What's wrong?*

Weigh your options and double-check your perspective to reach logical conclusions and make (one or more) workable decisions.

Warrior: *Take a risk and follow through.*

Plan your attack. Check your provisions. Take a deep breath. Go!

It's easy to make quick decisions based on minimal knowledge and a limited perspective. You can't effectively problem-solve without 1) finding all the information you need, 2) looking at possible solutions from different viewpoints, 3) making a well thought-out decision, and 4) going for your goal. By personifying the creative roles of Explorer, Artist, Judge, and Warrior, this model is an easy way to remember the four steps needed to reach valid, purposeful, and sometimes unusual choices and decisions.

Roger von Oech designed this model of creative thinking when he worked as a marketing representative for a computer company. He saw that many of his co-workers missed a lot of good ideas because they weren't looking for them. In 1977 he started his own consulting firm, designed to stimulate creativity and innovation in business. This model is great for anyone who wants to be more productive and more open-minded.

....

If you don't execute your ideas, they die.

Roger von Oech, creativity consultant & author

....

How can von Oech's method of creative thinking help with your college search?

You are The Creative Super-Hero!

As The Brave and Bold Explorer, you travel in minuscule airplanes, monstrous SUVs, and your own laptop to new and exciting places, searching in huge cities, scrambling through the sunny suburbs, investigating fertile farmland, and climbing high mountaintops to collect lots and lots and lots of information about colleges...

Now you're The Imaginative Artist, stirring up and swirling The Explorer's information in novel ways, creating ideas with an open and inquiring mind, asking original and insightful questions about where and where and why and how and what if, visualizing yourself as a student at each school...

As The Stalwart Judge you examine and weigh The Explorer's amazing discoveries and The Artist's unique interpretations. What colleges work for who you are? Which don't work? Is there enough evidence to warrant a valid judgment at this time? If not, you go back to the drawing board to gather and play with more ideas. When you find sufficient support, declare the verdict: where you'll apply to college...

All hail The Great Warrior! You go forward into the world of college applications, steeled with determination. You overcome obstacles that aren't obstacles when you look at them with courage and clarity (especially your essays). Rejected by some schools, you forge ahead to others. You're accepted to colleges that meet your needs, schools you really like!

(Drum roll, please...)

Your work as The Creative Super Hero is a creative college success!

Changing roles is a unique and valuable technique for creative thinking. You may enjoy it, you might think it's silly; but now that you've visualized von Oech's four characters, you'll remember the four steps to success in any area: information (Explorer), ideas (Artist), decisions (Judge), and action (Warrior).

Go forth and conquer!

For Your Consideration, a Condensed Consultation on…
Tony Buzan's Mind Maps

A Mind Map is a visual tool that helps you organize and remember information, and use your imagination to create new ideas and connections.

Say you're taking a class about pizza. Each session focuses on a different stage of pizza-making, including topics like making dough, choosing toppings, baking options, serving techniques, personal preferences, and customer opinions. How would you make a Mind Map about pizza class?

- Start by drawing a shape in the center of the paper that represents the main subject: in this case, "Pizza."

- Create lines coming from the central shape ("Pizza") for all the topics in the course: one line for "Ingredients," one for "Method of Cooking," one for "My Personal Preferences," and so on.

- Have new ideas or new information? Link them to other branches: from "Ingredients" springs a branch for "Cheese." "Cheese" branches out to "Mozzarella," "Cheddar," "Parmesan," "Feta."

- Draw more branches from each type of cheese: from "Mozzarella" pops "Smoked Mozzarella," "Fresh Mozzarella," and any other mozzarella you can think of.

- If you like an ingredient, connect it: "Smoked Mozzarella" links to "My Personal Preferences," along with "Proscuitto" from the "Meats" line.

- Oops! Forgot a line for "Crust." Connect it to the original "Pizza."

- Keep going: the possibilities are endless.

By drawing a Pizza Mind Map, you have just made connections and learned the important information that will be on the class final. You may also have created a completely new and delicious pizza: imagine a square prosciutto and smoked mozzarella on a pesto crust, grilled and slathered with olive oil and garlic. Yum.

When creating a Map, include flowing lines, few words, lots of color, and small drawings related to the idea. If you'd rather not draw, make a collage. Find photos or illustrations that go with your ideas and paste them on your Map. If you are having trouble making connections when you're drawing, visualize a Mind Map as a web site, clicking on links that connect to related links. Design your Map in a style that suits you.

Tony Buzan created the Mind Map while he was in college. He hated taking notes in class and saw that drawing and visually connecting information improved both his memory and his understanding of the material. He believes that our minds have a power of creativity that we don't use or develop. Our educational system needs to teach children how to be creative before we teach them what to learn. Buzan has written over eighty books about the creative mind, published in over one hundred countries.

· ·

Learning how to learn is life's most important skill.

Tony Buzan (1942-) educational consultant & author

· ·

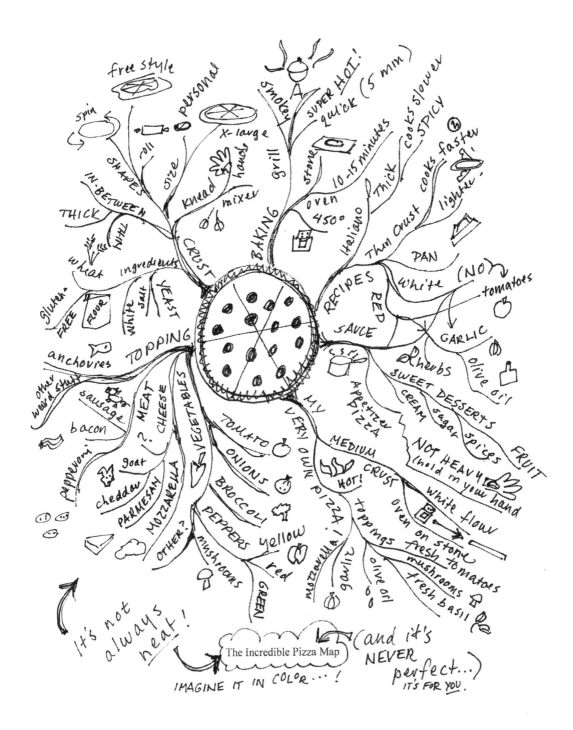

The Incredible Pizza Map

What do Buzan's Mind Maps have to do with college?

One valuable use of a Map is playing with ideas for your application essay. Make the central shape "Essay," branch out with possible topics and details about each. Why is that theme important, interesting, descriptive, relevant, funny, or serious? Who or what is the focus? What will it tell your reader about who you are? After you've had a chance to look at this brainstorming Map, make new Maps for each of the topics that look promising. Visualizing as you map makes it easier to come up with ideas, elaborate on them, narrow down your choices, and start writing your essay. (Does that remind of von Oech's four creative characters?)

Mind Mapping can also help you when you're looking at colleges, by identifying and organizing information, recognizing problems, and realizing possibilities. Draw your own college Map. Write the name of the school in the center. The first set of branches should show your basic interests and concerns, like academics, price, location, or dormitories. From each of these branches spring your own observations, opinions, and ideas.

Drawing Maps for all the schools you're considering offers a consistent means of comparison. Say you visited and/or researched eight different colleges and made a Map for each. Spread out all eight on a table or on the floor. Look at the "Application" branch and compare the schools' deadlines, essays, recommendations, and test scores. Contrast their academics. What majors do they offer? Are instructors mostly graduate students or are they professors? What's the school's grading system? If you're interested in specific "Departments," you can evaluate the classes and seminars they offer, the number of students in that department, and programs like semester abroad. Practical branch considerations are important, too: Colleges A and G have excellent food service; B has lousy food. Colleges C, F, and G are closest to home; College H is the farthest away. Seeing the differences between schools helps you make choices and, sometimes, compromises.

Give Mind Mapping a try and look at both essays and college connections from a different perspective. If you're not comfortable with drawing, try creating your Map in a different way. No one has to see it but you. Remember what Howard Gardner said about developing all eight of your abilities?

Tony Buzan agrees.

ATM or Slot Machine

ATM: An acronym for *Automated Teller Machine*: a banking machine activated by a customer entering a PIN (*Personal Identification Number*). The customer may then perform basic banking services, including withdrawing cash, depositing checks, checking account balances, or transferring funds.

An ATM can be found at banks, stores, and other public places.
An ATM is predictable. You insert your card, type in your personal code and how much money you want. The machine dispenses that exact amount of money.

Slot Machine: A gambling machine operated by person inserting coins or tokens into a slot. When the button is pushed or the handle is pulled, a set of three or more spinning symbols are displayed. The final alignment of these symbols determines whether the player wins any money or not.

A slot machine can only be found in a gambling casino.
A slot machine is unpredictable. You insert your coin or token, push the button or pull the handle, and cash may, or may not, be dispensed. Your winnings or losses depend totally on chance.

How are the ATM and a Slot Machine different?

An ATM gives you your money from your own bank account.
A slot machine gives you the casino's (i.e. other players') money.

An ATM…

A slot machine…

An ATM…

A slot machine…

An ATM…

A slot machine…

How are the ATM and the slot machine similar?

Both dispense money.
Both are made of metal.
Both have flashing electric lights.

Both…

Both…

Both…

ATM can also be an acronym for *Academically Talented and Motivated*, referring to those students who are consistently successful in school.

How are ATM students like an ATM machine?

An ATM machine…

ATM students…

An ATM machine…

ATM students…

An ATM machine…

ATM students…

Slot machines might apply to those students who perform inconsistently in school. Their work is sometimes just okay or, other times, exceptional.

How are slot machine students like a slot machine?

A slot machine…

Slot machine students…

A slot machine…

Slot machine students…

A slot machine…

Slot machine students…

Will your style of thinking as an ATM, a slot machine, or both, influence your college search?

Inventions of the Fun and Creative Kind by Creative and Fun Inventors Twiz

*Use The Clues to find all your toys
and you'll find the magical quote you seek!*

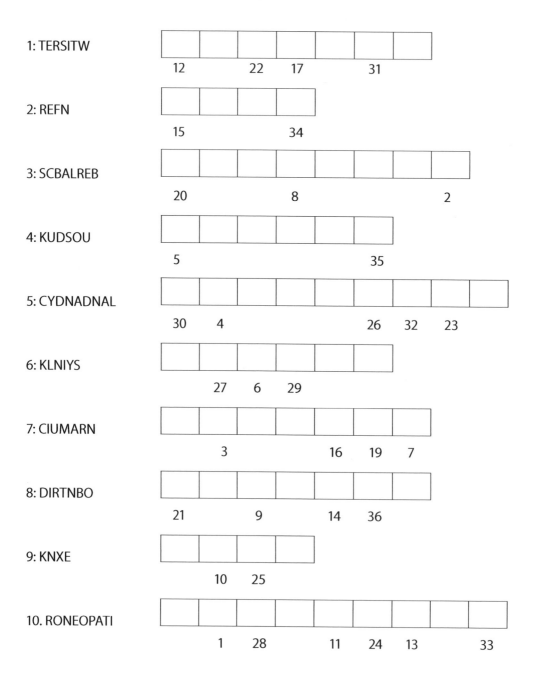

1: TERSITW

12   22   17   31

2: REFN

15   34

3: SCBALREB

20   8   2

4: KUDSOU

5   35

5: CYDNADNAL

30   4   26   32   23

6: KLNIYS

27   6   29

7: CIUMARN

3   16   19   7

8: DIRTNBO

21   9   14   36

9: KNXE

10   25

10. RONEOPATI

1   28   11   24   13   33

The Clues:

1: "Be flexible!" Reyn Geyer
   Dartmouth College (NH), Journalism

2: "Ouch! Not." (the same) Reyn Geyer
   Dartmouth College (NH), Journalism

3: "To the letter!" Alfred Butts
   University of Pennsylvania, Architecture

4: "To the number!" Howard Garns
   University of Illinois, Architectural Engineering

5: "Watch out for that witch!" Eleanor Abbott
   Radcliff College (MA: formerly the women's college of Harvard University), Education

6: "Boing!" Richard James
   Pennsylvania State University, Mechanical Engineering

7: "My brain hurts!" Richard Tait
   Heriot Watt University (Scotland), Computer Science

8: "Please connect me!" Tim Walsh
   Colgate University (NY), Art and Art History

9: "Make it snappy!" Joel Glickman
   Syracuse University (NY), Fine Arts

10: "Excuse me, do you have your insurance card?" John Spinello
    University of Illinois, Industrial Design

Turn the page and solve the puzzle!

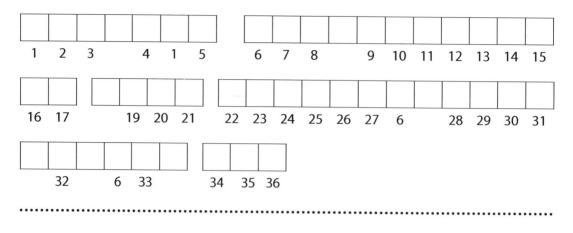

1	2	3		4	1	5

6 7 8   9 10 11 12 13 14 15

16 17   19 20 21   22 23 24 25 26 27 6   28 29 30 31

32   6 33   34 35 36

· ·

George Scialabba (1948-) book critic

· ·

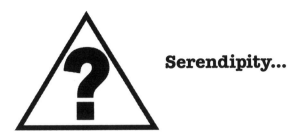 **Serendipity...**

What if your expensive cell phone fell into a fish tank full of expensive piranhas?

If you could hear what someone is thinking for a day, who would you choose?

What if dogs were as dumb as chickens, but chickens were as smart as chimpanzees?

Why is it that when someone tells you that there are
billions of stars in the universe, you believe her?
But if she tells you the paint on the wall is wet, you have to touch it?

If you try to fail, and succeed, which have you done?

Chapter 3
The Business of College

"… and now a word from our sponsor."

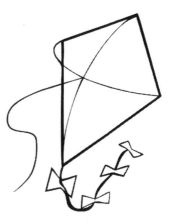

....

Drive thy business, let not that drive thee.

Benjamin Franklin (1706-1790) statesman, printer & inventor

....

You've found the perfect job with a perfect company. It's exactly what you want to do, in a great location, and you're totally qualified.

You send in an application and you're called for an interview.

The interview goes really well. The interviewer is obviously impressed with both your resume and you as a person. She tells you they're making decisions next week, you seem like an excellent candidate, and it was a pleasure to meet you.

You go home and write a note to the interviewer thanking her for her time, how impressed you are with the company, and how your qualifications and experience will benefit the business.

You sit back and exhale. You're sure they'll hire you.

You wait. A week goes by. "Maybe they haven't had time to finalize my contract," you think.

Another week goes by and you still haven't heard anything.

You finally decide to call the interviewer just to check up on your status. She says, "Oh, I'm so sorry we didn't contact you. We filled that position last week. I'll be sure we keep your application on file if we have another opening."

You're in shock. That job was perfect for you and you were perfect for the job. What do you do?

It's obvious. You look for another job.
Hmmm… why does this sound familiar?

College is lot like a business. Both use applications and interviews for screening. They look at the quality of your experience, and make decisions about whether you're accepted or rejected. The cultural explosion of technology and media allows competitive colleges to attract students through clever advertising, constant promotion, free publicity, concerned Public Relations, increased sales, and effective marketing. What do these business strategies do for a college? They help colleges find the right students for their school.

Will you be hired or fired?

....

A business exists to create a customer.

Peter F. Drucker (1909-2005) writer & management consultant

....

What is Business anyway?

....

If the circus is coming to town and you paint
a sign saying "Circus Coming to the Fairground
on Saturday," that's Advertising.

If you put the sign on the back of an elephant
and walk it into town, that's Promotion.

If the elephant walks through the mayor's
flowerbed, that's Publicity.

And if you get the mayor to laugh about it,
that's Public Relations.

If the town's citizens go the circus, you show them the
many entertainment booths, explain how much fun they'll have spending
money at the booths, answer their questions and
ultimately, they spend a lot at the circus, that's Sales.

And, if you planned the whole thing, that's Marketing!

Author Unknown

....

This clever quip sums up how to run a successful business. What does that have to do with college? College is a business. Factors like shrinking endowments, governmental budget cuts, less money to pay employees, and increased costs of facility maintenance has raised the cost and the expectations of higher education. Well-known schools know that a strong reputation is essential for their college's media ranking. Parents want to know that that an exclusive college is providing the education and the life-style that they're paying for. Higher college rankings + happy students = more money for the school. Lesser-known colleges may believe that a bigger and better image will draw more and better students to the school. More positive publicity + more students = more money for the school.

A successful business uses all of these "circus" strategies: Advertising, Promotion, Publicity, Public Relations, Sales, and Marketing. If the business of college is to be successful, they need to use them, too.

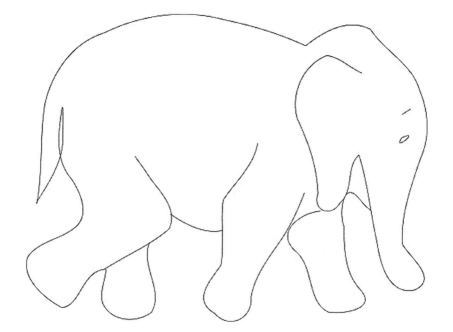

Advertising *AKA The Circus Sign*

"Did you see that sign? The circus is at the Fairgrounds! Let's go on Saturday!"

A "target audience" is a select group of people that a business wants as consumers. Advertising presents their product or services as more desirable than competing products to that target audience. For example, teenagers and senior citizens would be different targets. You probably wouldn't see an ad for the best, strongest denture adhesive on the online sites you frequent. Your grandparents probably wouldn't see ads for the best, strongest caffeinated energy drink on the TV shows they watch. An effective advertising campaign creates a recognizable identity for a specific product for a specific target group: you see the logo, you hear the slogan, and you can instantly identify and "know" it's the best product for you.

Every college or university has to advertise. No logo, no slogan, no recognition leads to no applications. They must project the idea that their school is as good, if not better, than any other school of its size, location, or status. If you didn't see the sign that said the circus was coming to town this weekend and where it will be, how would you know when it was or where to go? If you didn't know a particular college existed, how would you know to look or apply there?

You, as a potential college student, are an official member of the advertiser's target audience.

Promotion *AKA The Walking Elephant*

Look at me! I'm the Unusual Elephant! My circus has logo t-shirts, sweatshirts, sweatpants, shorts, fleece, uniforms, car stickers, car magnets, key chains, picture frames, beer mugs, coffee mugs, wine glasses, baseball hats, knit hats, pins, ties, underwear, stuffed animals, pencils, pens, mouse pads, baby clothes, posters, jewelry, socks, flags, tickets to concessions, tickets to the tiger performance, and tickets to free arcade games!

Look at me! I'm the Usual College Store! My college has logo t-shirts, sweatshirts, sweatpants, shorts, fleece, uniforms, car stickers, car magnets, key chains, picture frames, beer mugs, coffee mugs, wine glasses, baseball hats, knit hats, pins, ties, underwear, stuffed animals, pencils, pens, mouse pads, baby clothes, posters, jewelry, socks, flags, tickets to concerts, tickets to comedy performances, and tickets to football games!

Promotion is key to any business. A college wants you to know they're out there. Ultimately it's your choice to participate in the promotion of a school: "What a great, high-quality T-shirt!

I'm buying them for everyone in my family!" "They're raffling tickets to the concert!" "They're giving away tickets to the game!" "They're randomly choosing students for free tickets to the concert and a free dinner!" In sharing the products and opportunities of a college with others, you publicly endorse that school.

So who's the real promoter? You are, proudly wearing that great, high-quality T-shirt with your favorite college's logo on the front.

Publicity *AKA The Flowerbed*
The town was buzzing when they heard that the elephant stepped in the mayor's flowerbed. But on the positive side, now everyone knew that the circus was in town!

Publicists may work with one person or a thousand. They relay information through media: print, mailings, and online. They handle new information that the media has released with or without their approval. It's often said that any publicity is good publicity. When a reputable news source reports that a celebrity has contributed personal and financial support to a political, environmental, or artistic cause, you see that person as a kind and generous. Tabloid magazines always write about some scandalous celebrity. You read the article in the grocery line or the dentist's office and remember that person and his negative antics for a long time. Can that scandalous star in the tabloids change his image by suddenly supporting an important public issue, too? Will you now see him as kind and generous? His publicist would orchestrate it of course. Good or bad, it's publicity!

Colleges need publicity to attract applicants. When the media covers student participation in community service or alumni support of a worthy cause, the public sees that college as caring and authentic. Sometimes a negative or frightening event occurs on campus and word gets out to the media quickly. Immediate action of the college, like tightening security, changing ineffective policies, or getting involved in fundraising for related issues, creates better public perception of the school. Effective publicity strategies can both promote the college's achievements and spin a negative situation into a positive change.

Schools want and need you to remember them in a positive light, and the media can help. You, your parents, and the local and world community are a publicist's target audience.

Public Relations *AKA The Laughing Mayor*
If the Mayor is laughing, it must be okay that his flowerbed is ruined. Don't worry. We can fix it!

Public Relations representatives work for business clients by assessing and solving consumer needs and concerns via research, surveys, and action plans. Their goal is to create a positive and productive relationship within the organization and with the business target audience.

Colleges have the same goals as those in business: to assess and address concerns, establish good media relations and public understanding of the school's objectives, and help make the school population positive and productive. PR people plan campus events like environmental workshops, sponsoring community service programs, offering seminars about the arts, and organizing activities that promote specific student interests. They also provide pro-active community support to the campus and neighboring areas when something bad happens: devastating acts of nature like a hurricane or a flood, or tragic human actions like campus shootings.

The mission of Public Relations at a college is to make everyone on campus feel comfortable in a safe and giving community. PR's safe and giving college community welcomes you to their comfortable target audience.

Sales *AKA The Spending Citizens*
At the circus the crowd is excited and ready to have fun. If you can attract them with what the circus offers that they couldn't find anywhere else, you can easily make a sale. Who wouldn't want to play the booth games to win a prize? Where else can you enjoy a super-jumbo stick of blue cotton candy? Oh, and don't forget to ride on the Ferris wheel!

How does a business attract buyers? They find their target audience and convince them that they need to buy their product. Colleges have to use the same strategy in order to attract applicants. With all the other schools out there, a college needs to stand out as unique, relevant, and a good financial deal. A college representative will tell you what the school can give you that others can't. A school may offer excellent academic or sports programs that other colleges don't. Perhaps it's an appealing location that offers beaches or mountains or a city. You may want a school with an established national reputation, or maybe a school that's also admirable but less competitive. You might need a college that offers more financial aid or merit scholarships or lower tuition. Whatever you're looking for, there's a college that provides what you want and need. You in turn are providing that college what they need to keep going: tuition.

You and your parents, spending money for college via savings, loans, financial aid, scholarships, or your great-grandfather's trust fund, are the saleable target audience.

Marketing *AKA The Plan*
The "you planned it all" at the circus means "you did it all." You put up the sign, brought the elephant, fixed the mayor's flowerbed, got him laugh about it, and made a lot of money for the business.

You've successfully performed the classic marketing model, the "4 P's:" Product, Price, Placement, and Promotions. You presented a unique idea in a memorable way (Product), set up a range of customer income (Price), identified a target audience and their specific need for the product (Placement), and worked to get the undivided attention of that target audience (Promotions).

Colleges do the same thing. Schools usually handle their marketing campaign by hiring an outside agency. By gathering high school students' academic information, an agency can locate a target market. Direct marketing experts can look at your online history, the sites you visit and when, what you purchase, and who you talk to. This information may determine whether you're the kind of student the college is looking for, where you want to go to go to school, how much money you have to pay tuition, and what it would take to get you to apply.

Even a school's website is designed to define, reflect, and sell their college's "personality." One site has bright colors with wording in a casual font (unconventional school); another uses traditional jewel-tones and classic fonts (established school). One profiles students partying at a football game (fun school), while another shows students in a high-tech science lab (academically focused school). Which site is appealing to a person like you? The marketing people already know.

So who's the target audience? You are. Welcome to the circus of business!

Have you seen colleges use these business strategies? How?

Does your high school use these business strategies? How?

The Business Application

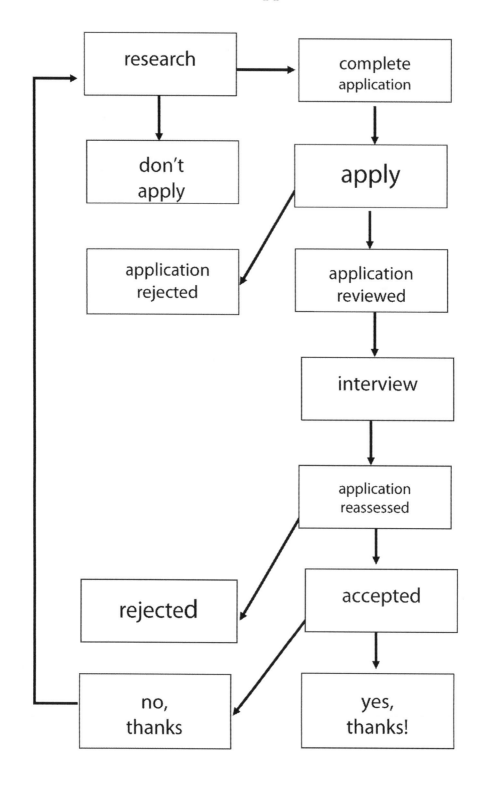

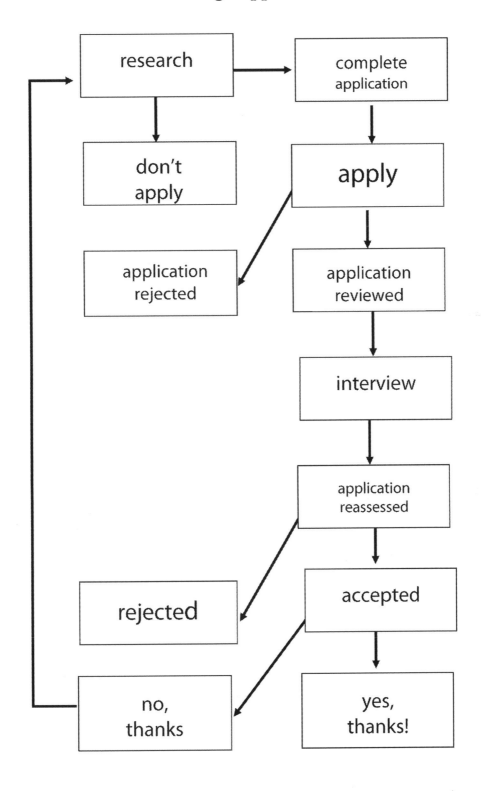

The College Application

INTERVIEW: Business Tips

1. Be on time.

2. Dress appropriately.

3. Don't chew gum.

4. Don't wear too much cologne or perfume.

5. Smile.

6. Prepare to answer a lot of questions, like "What are your goals?" "Why are you interested in working here?"

7. Prepare to ask a lot of well thought-out questions, like "I understand you offer some interesting evening seminars. Can anyone attend, from any department?" or "I read that you have research positions. I'd like to know more about them."

8. Research before the interview and don't ask questions that could be answered from a brochure or on-line, like "How many departments do you have?"

9. Write a short thank you note right away. E-mail is fine, but a written note is a tad classier. Say how much you appreciated speaking with him/her, ask any questions you forgot to ask, and say again how interested you are. Proofread carefully before sending it out.

INTERVIEW: College Tips

1. Be on time.

2. Dress appropriately.

3. Don't chew gum.

4. Don't wear too much cologne or perfume.

5. Smile.

6. Prepare to answer a lot of questions, like "What are your goals?" "Why are you interested in coming here?"

7. Prepare to ask a lot of well thought-out questions, like "I understand you offer some interesting evening seminars. Can anyone attend, from any department?" or "I read that you have research positions. I'd like to know more about them."

8. Research before the interview and don't ask questions that could be answered from a brochure or on-line, like "How many departments do you have?"

9. Write a short thank you note right away. E-mail is fine, but a written note is a tad classier. Say how much you appreciated speaking with him/her, ask any questions you forgot to ask, and say again how interested you are. Proofread carefully before sending it out.

Business chooses employees like colleges choose students.

Applying for a job does not mean you're going to be hired. Submitting an application to a college does not guarantee admission. Even if the interviewer loved you, the school may have specific criteria that the school must meet at the time. It may not seem fair, but that's business. At any given time, an organization may need employees or students with certain qualities and assets:

Strong Work/Academic Records

Business: "We need employees with the best previous work experience."

College: "We need applicants with the best possible classroom and test performance."

Special Talents

Business: "This quarter it looks like we need to hire a manager, a computer specialist, and a graphic designer."

College: "This school year it looks like we need to find an ice hockey goalie, a bass player, and a published poet."

Community/Social Service

Business: "We're looking for applicants who have experience in promoting team-building, planning departmental conferences, or serving on social committees."

College: "We're looking for applicants who have experience in establishing new clubs, planning on-campus speakers and concerts, or leading student government."

Geographic Diversity

Business: "Looking at our present demographics, we need to diversify and balance our employee pool by hiring candidates from different geographic regions, sex, race, religion, or culture."

College: "Looking at our present demographics, we need to diversify and balance our student body by accepting applicants from different geographic regions, sex, race, religion, or culture."

Special Needs

Business: "We need to support our employees with benefits that address physical handicaps and personal, health, or financial problems."

College: "We need to support our students with programs that address physical handicaps, learning disabilities, or bad financial situations."

Your extracurricular activities, your standardized test scores, and your GPA may be perfectly suited to a college, but you may not be the kind of student a particular college is looking for right now. Nothing personal. On the other hand, a school might be searching for someone just like you. If you don't apply, you'll never know.

College Marketing...

What if you went to the mailbox and found a completely unsolicited, personalized-with-your-name-in-embossed-letters college application sent directly to you? No essay! No application fee! Sign it and send it back! You're officially in the pool of contenders for that school.

Your mail-in application is a "fast-track application," produced through direct-marketing firms for colleges across the country. Eligible students are chosen by their standardized test scores and other high school information, purchased from respectable college sources. Some schools who fast-track are "brand-name," some lesser known. But all participating colleges report more applicants than they're ever received in the past. One college sent out 40,000 fast-track applications in 2010 for a freshman class of about 1900 students.

Critics of fast-track applications say that because "it's free!" advertising draws in a larger number of applicants, a school will rate higher in published college rankings. Get more applicants; reject more applicants. They also suggest that because fast-tracks are so easy to submit, students may choose schools that really aren't right for them.

Proponents of fast-tracking say that this marketing strategy increases a college's visibility; many students haven't heard of the school until they receive the application in the mail. More applicants mean the school has a broader selection of candidates, especially those students who can't afford application fees. The diversity of applicants, by region, race, ethnicity, and gender, builds a more balanced school community.

Who do you think is right?

Brand Names...

You're visiting a college. Your parents are in a parent orientation session, so you're on your own for an hour. You really want a cup of coffee. There's coffee in the college food court, but you had it when you got here this morning and it wasn't great. You head down the street and after a couple of blocks you see a little coffee shop on the left. It has a funky, artistic sign, little tables outside, and baked goods in the front window. You start walking toward it when the national coffee chain you were virtually raised on appears directly across the street. Let's call the brand name chain "Coffee Y," and the local café, "Coffee Z."

You recognized the bright green logo above Coffee Y right away. You know their high reputation for popular products and good service. It's kind of cool that they don't advertise on TV, only on their website and in print. All their stores have WiFi, clean bathrooms, comfortable seating, and those delicious blueberry muffins you like. Their coffee is pricey, but you know what you're getting: predictably good coffee.

You don't know anything about Coffee Z. The space looks nice, but you've never seen it advertised, and the tour guide on campus didn't mention it. Do they have WiFi? Is their seating comfortable? Are the bathrooms clean? Do they have good blueberry muffins? Most important, how's their coffee?

You trust Coffee Y. But Coffee Z might be really good.

Where <u>should</u> you go to get coffee?

Where <u>would</u> you go to get coffee?

Are brand names better?

What does this have to do with choosing a college?

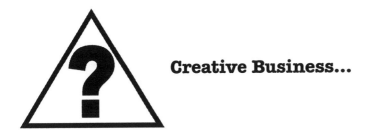

Creative Business...

The Association of American Colleges and Universities commissioned Hart Research Associates to ask employers what colleges should teach in order to create more effective and successful employees. Among the seventeen choices given in the employer survey, the highest rated were: written and oral communication (89%), critical thinking and analytical reasoning (81%), and complex problem solving (75%). Creativity and innovation (70%) was ranked in the top eight of the seventeen.

Raising the Bar: Employers' Views on College Learning in the Wake of the Economic Downturn, A Survey Among Employers Conducted on Behalf of The Association of American Colleges and Universities by Hart Research Associates, 2010

What are the benefits of being creative in business?

What are the benefits of being creative in college?

The Big Biz Twiz

Successful business people have determination, persistence, and very good PR. Who's in what business?

a.   Seattle's hot CEO Howard Schultz makes a fortune in the morning.
        Northern Michigan University: Communications

b.   Clothing magnate Donald Fisher has bridged young fashion for generations.
        University of California-Berkley: Business Administration

c.   Light on his feet, Phil Knight just does it.
        University of Oregon: Accounting

d.   TV queen Oprah Winfrey turned her name around.
        Tennessee State University: Communications

e.   Cable TV's Judy McGrath raised the pulse of the nation.
        Cedar Crest College (PA): English

f.   Crafty Martha Stewart has a hand in everything, everywhere.
        Barnard College (CT): European and Architectural History

g.   Jerry Greenfield got the chilly scoop with puns and celebrities.
        Oberlin College (OH): Pre-Med

h.   "Papa" John Schnatter always spins a savory bite or two.
        Ball State University (IN): Business

i.   Sheryl Sandberg has millions of people looking in the mirror 24/7.
        Harvard University (MA): Economics

j.   Web-savvy Carol Bartz expresses her delight in technology every day.
        University of Wisconsin–Madison: Computer Science

1. Papa John's Pizza, *founded in 1984, based in Louisville KY*

2. Ben and Jerry's Ice Cream, *founded in 1978 in Burlington VT*

3. Facebook, *established in 2004 in Cambridge MA*

4. MTV, *established in 1981 in NY NY*

5. Living Omnimedia, *founded in 1997 in NY NY*

6. Yahoo!, *founded in 1995 in Santa Clara CA*

7. Nike, *founded in 1964 in Portland OR*

8. Gap, *founded in 1969 in San Francisco CA*

9. Starbucks, *established in 1971 in Seattle WA*

10. Harpo Productions, *founded in 1986 in Chicago IL*

(Personal Space. Creative Business vs. Creative College.)

Chapter 4
Finding Schools

Too Many Choices, So Little Time

....

It's not what you look at that matters, it's what you see.

Henry Davis Thoreau (1817-1862) author & naturalist

....

Today you're shopping for a pair of jeans.

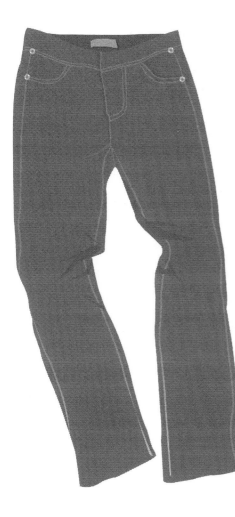

Where would you look?

O Designer store
O Department store
O Discount store
O Used clothing store
O Online

What's most important to you?

O Style
O Price
O Fabric
O Brand
O Comfort

How many pairs would you be willing to try on to find a pair you'd buy?

O 1-2
O 3-5
O 6-8
O 9-12
O as many as it takes

Someone is shopping with you. What could they say that would make you want to buy a certain pair?

- ○ "You look really good in those. Turn around."
- ○ "They're on sale! Buy them.""
- ○ "You look like a rock star, baby!"
- ○ "They are sooo worth the money."
- ○ Nothing. If you don't like them, you're not buying them.

Someone is shopping with you. What could they say that would make you decide <u>not</u> to buy a certain pair?

- ○ "I'm not sure. Turn around."
- ○ "They're having a sale next week. Maybe you should just wait."
- ○ "They look sort of like something my 9 year-old cousin would wear."
- ○ "They're really kind of cheap looking."
- ○ Nothing. If you like them, you're buying them.

You found a pair you like. Would you buy them?

- ○ Yes. They look perfect.
- ○ Yes. They're a great price.
- ○ Yes. Buy them, but keep the tags on for a few days in case you change your mind.
- ○ No. Put them back. You can probably find a better buy somewhere else.
- ○ No. Put them back. You decide you really don't need new jeans right now.

Do you choose a pair of jeans because of price? Looks? Practicality? What would other people think of your shopping decisions? You make these decisions every day: when you get a new cell phone, decide what restaurant you'll go to, determine what house you'll rent for senior week, and, of course, when you're buying clothes. You may mentally process options quickly, or sometimes too quickly, based on your personal opinions and priorities.

We're all creatures of habit and sometimes we lose out because we only choose what we know. Becoming more aware of who you are and why you make certain choices will help you make more solid decisions. Sometimes clothes look better on a hanger than they do on you. Sometimes you find clothes that don't look great on the hanger, only to find they're perfect for you. Try on more than one pair of jeans, look in the mirror and see them from all angles before you decide to buy one. Or two. Or ten.

Looking at colleges and choosing a college major work the same way. Choosing where you want to spend the next four years can be scary. What if you make a mistake? Would it ruin the rest of your life?

Relax. You don't have to buy anything right away.

Where's that dressing room with the three-way mirror?

. . . .

Know, first, who you are; and then adorn yourself accordingly.

Epictetus (AD 55–AD 135) Greek philosopher

. . . .

How to start looking for colleges

Buy or borrow one or two where-to-go college guides.
This a cultural prerequisite for a college search. They have some good information about schools they've selected, and some include student opinions. Just remember that not all schools are listed or included. Does that matter to you? You decide.

Go to a college fair.
High schools usually host a college fair for juniors in the spring. Admission representatives each have a table for their college with information about their school. The colleges you like might not be represented, but it's good to see what else is out there. Collect the school catalogs to go over later.

Go to Guidance sessions hosting visiting college representatives.
Some college admission representatives or alumni visit high schools to speak with students interested in their school. These small group sessions are good opportunities to gather information, talk about opportunities, and ask specific questions about the college. (You may have to miss a class, but you can certainly suffer through it.)

Schedule a meeting with your Guidance Counselor.
Your Guidance Counselor gathers all your paperwork, makes sure your test scores go to the right schools, writes you a required letter of reference, checks that your applications are complete, and mails them all off to the right admissions offices before their deadlines. Schedule a meeting early in the school year so your counselor at least knows your face when writing letters about you and shuffling your papers. Knowing you as a person can help your counselor make better suggestions about schools for you. As a rule, Guidance Counselors don't bite. But if a student they don't know comes into their office for help the afternoon before applications are due, they might.

Use Guidance software.
Some high schools have computer software that provides you with organizational tools, keeps track of your search process, and lists colleges that might work for you. For some people a program like this is a great way to stay on track. However, it does require a commitment to enter new data regularly. Sci-fi computers in movies know absolutely everything about everything, including you. The software in the Guidance Office knows only programmed and objective information about you. Just remember that the software's college choices are only suggestions.

Save everything from colleges that comes in the mail or email.
You are about to be (or are already) barraged with information about colleges.

Find three containers: boxes, trash bags, grocery bags, old pillowcases. It doesn't matter what you use as long as can they can hold a lot. When you receive a college mailing or email, take a quick look at the school sending it. You don't have to read it right away. You're creating a collection.

- If you've heard about the school and it looks interesting, put it in the first container: Container #1.

- If you've heard of the school but you're not interested, put it in the second container: Container #2.

- If you've never heard of the school, put it in the third container: Container #3.

- Go through these books, brochures, and printouts when you have time. After reading their information you may find that a Container #1 school that you thought you liked belongs in Container #2: you really don't want to apply there. If you like a school that you hadn't heard of before and are now interested in, move it from #3 into #1… and so on.

- Re-read their Container #1 promotional material before visiting that college. You'll have a lot of data and can prepare to ask good questions.

Go online to look at schools.
A college's site gives you direct information about who they are and what they can do for you. Check out the visuals and language of the site. What's their marketing strategy? What kind of student are they trying to attract? Are you in their target market? If so, start researching and possibly schedule a tour. There are also private websites that focus on student reviews for a number of colleges and universities. Some campus participants produce their own college tour videos, which may give you a different view of what students consider important. Keep in mind that students who like their school are going to be positive about "their" school.

Draw your visit.
Make copies of your own college Mind Map formatted with your own relevant branches. That way you can easily put Maps from other schools side by side to compare the facts and your

impressions. Don't forget to add branches when you find something unusual or interesting at a school. Keep pencils and paper in your car or your backpack.

Record your visit.

When you visit a new school, relying on memory alone won't help much when deciding whether to apply to that school or not. The Fact/Opinion sheets on the following pages can help you remember what you saw, heard, and experienced while visiting. The first form is an objective review of school information. You can fill it out with what you already know or ask your guide questions when you're on the tour. The second sheet is for your personal opinions and impressions while you're on the visit: observations, interpretation, and priorities. Make copies of the Fact/Opinion sheets and keep them in your backpack or in your car. You never know when you'll come across a school you like.

Visit local colleges with friends.

If a friend says he's going to see a college nearby, ask if you can come along. Share your impressions on during the tour and on your way home. It's always interesting to see how a friend's opinions and priorities compare to your own, especially when making college choices. After all, you don't like same pizza; do you have to like the same schools?

Visit colleges with family.

Map out a road trip and be open-minded. Visit the schools you think you'll like, some you're not sure about, and one or two your parents suggest. You might be pleasantly surprised. Driving through Boston to visit your grandmother? Ask your parents if you can take an extra hour and drop in at one of the many colleges there. The college may even give you an unscheduled private tour and a free lunch.

Be open-minded about where to look at colleges.

....

I think it is important to give kids the opportunity to see all
types of schools, urban, rural, big, small, close to home and even
international. My parents and I made many special trips to places where
they thought that I would like to look at schools, knowing that I wanted
to be in a large city atmosphere. They did make me go on several tours of
schools that I was not interested in that were in smaller towns, etc., but in
retrospect it was good to get a comparison. I am glad that they made some
decisions as to where to look at schools, otherwise I would have never
thought to visit some of the campuses we looked at.

Maris, Editorial Assistant for a national magazine
Undergraduate Degree in English

....

....

One never goes so far as when one doesn't know where one is going.

Johann Wolfgang von Goethe (1749–1832) poet, writer & scientist

....

College:	FACTS & INFORMATION
Location	
Public or Private	
Undergraduate Enrollment	
Student/ Faculty Ratio	
Qualifying SAT/ACT Scores	
School's Known Curriculum Strengths	
School Scholarships	
Common Application (Y/N)	
School Application (Y/N)	
Interview (Y/N)	
Early Decision or Early Action (Y/N)	
Application Deadlines	
Application Fee	
Price of Housing and Food Plans	
Tuition	

College:	OPINIONS
Competitive, serious, or laid back?	
Intriguing classes in possible majors?	
Variety of interesting elective classes?	
Do students look happy?	
Nice campus?	
Nice dorms?	
Good food?	
Weather?	
Shopping nearby?	
Free on-campus transportation?	
Fun school extracurricular activities?	
Fun non-school extracurricular activities?	
Transportation to get home and back?	
Anything else?	
Apply or not?	

Three opinions, five questions.
What do you think?

A College Counselor's View

You're a unique individual. You need to find a college that fits you.

Should I visit all the schools I'm considering?

Some students prefer to visit lots of schools, then apply. Others wait until they're accepted, then visit the schools on their short list.

Discuss this with your parents, since they'll be tagging along. Time and budgets permitting (can you really visit the University of Hawaii if you live in New York?) it's a good idea to visit at least a few schools the summer after your junior year to get an idea of what you like... and don't like... about certain types of schools: campuses, neighborhoods, size of school, location, student body. No pressure at this point... you're just window-shopping.

After acceptance, arrange a second, more in-depth visit to schools on your short list. Most schools have programs where you can shadow a current student; spend the night in his/her dorm room, attend classes, eat the cafeteria food, meet the people... be a college student for a day or two.

Should I interview?

Yes -- If the school conducts interviews, and if you feel it will help your chances of acceptance into a top choice school. Make sure your communications and interview skills are polished to make the most of that face time! Remember your appearance, good posture, direct eye contact and a firm handshake. All those things an adult probably has nagged you about are very important, especially for interviews. Anticipate the questions they might ask, and practice your answers. Treat the interview as if you were preparing for a test... *because you are.*

Does higher tuition mean it's a better school?

Of course... isn't everything better if it's more expensive? Seriously, students are getting tremendous educational value at all different levels of tuition; from community college to Ivy League. You need to discuss college budgets with your parents and focus your search reasonably. Keep in mind that posted tuition price is often reduced through scholarships, grants and loans, so a reach school may become "reachable" with the right amount of aid.

How many colleges should I apply to?

More than one; less than 20. Most experts suggest you include at least one school each in your "safety," "target," and "reach" profiles, so 3-9 applications are a reasonable figure.

Keep a few things in mind:

- Application fees will be the least expensive part of your college career, so if you're not certain, apply. Applying to a school increases your chances of acceptance 100% over those who do not apply.

- Apply to schools you would actually attend (because you might actually attend them.)

- There will always be more options; more schools, more suggestions to add to your decisions and perhaps make you second-guess your choices. When it's all said and done, you can only go to one school at a time... so don't make yourself crazy.

My dream school has the best program for my major. Can I improve my chance of admission?

There are a few steps you can take to improve your odds if you're a borderline candidate for your "dream school". Face it; colleges *want* to extend offers to students who *want* to go there-- so let them know they are your first choice in all of your communications.

Many schools weigh your interest by the number of "touch points" or times you've expressed interest in them. Without becoming a stalker, you can market yourself with the appropriate "touch points" of contacts and communication, such as:

- Incorporate the fact that they are your top choice in your essay

- Tell the college representative who visits your school or whom you meet at the college fair.

- Contact the college via email with any questions you have.

- Respect their busy schedules, and email only valid inquiries.

- Visit the school at least once: arrange for an interview if possible.

- Let the admissions officers know of your preference for their school. Ask for their business cards and follow up by email after your campus visit to thank them and continue to express your interest.

- If you have an extracurricular or athletic talent which may benefit the school, get in touch with the right coach or professor at the college to advocate you; if he/she needs a 200 meter sprinter or a tuba player and you fit the bill, that's a big plus.

- Apply early action or early decision. Many schools have more favorable admission rates to early decision candidates.

- Most importantly, have a plan B. Research, select and apply to a solid, second-choice safety school where you can succeed just in case.

Go where you will be happy, successful and will thrive, with a major in mind and the flexibility to change if moved to do so during your college experience. Enjoy the journey... as long as you graduate in 4 years. :>)

Leslie Adams, corporate Leadership and Communications consultant for Fortune 500 companies, believes that the best advice for a person looking for colleges is to be flexible and realistic. She has two sons who've gone through the college adventure.

··

Organizing is what you do before you do something,
so that when you do it, it is not all mixed up.

A. A. Milne (1882-1956) creator and author of Winnie-the-Pooh

··

Was the counselor's advice helpful? How? Why?

Do you agree with any part of the counselor's approach?

Do you disagree with any part of the counselor's approach?

A Behavioral Economic View

You're a unique individual. But what if you're not? Research in Behavioral Economics shows that human behavior is predictable, and many of the decisions we make aren't logical.

Should I visit all the colleges I'm considering?

Best choice: don't visit. Research the school, apply, and get accepted before going to see it. When you're visiting a campus for the first time, you'll form opinions that may or may not portray the school as a place you'd want to go. Tour guides, the food, the grounds, the classrooms and other factors might influence your decision. For instance, you might get an incredibly boring tour guide, but does that mean the college and all their programs are boring, too? If you had a fabulous guide at that same school, you'd be running to admissions and begging for an application. Think of visiting a college as a "first date": even if you have a great time, one date is not a valid reason to get married. A good visit is a good reason for a "second date" to further explore the territory before you commit. A bad visit? You won't be back.

The weather can influence your choice of colleges, too. A research group surveyed students on their experience visiting a chosen university. This school was rated high academically but lower on recreational programs. On a sunny day, visiting students focused on the school's lack of outdoor activities: "There's nothing to do here." On a cloudy day, potential students focused on academics: "There's even a history class on George Washington's wooden teeth!" When admitted to the school, which students were more likely to accept? The cloudy-day

75

visitors. Their memory of their visit was academic; the classrooms, the courses offered, the professors. They didn't know it, but those clouds helped them make a logical decision. After all, a school-sponsored ultimate Frisbee team would be great, but is that why you're going to college in the first place? If you go there you can start your own team.

Should I interview?
Unless a college requires an interview, don't offer. Meeting a person representing the school face-to-face creates emotional, not logical, first impressions. You don't like the interviewer, so you don't like the school. You love the interviewer, you love the school. (If your favorite cousin loves a school, will you love it, too? If the cousin you hate loves a school…?). But don't jeopardize your application; if the school insists that you interview, interview.

Does higher tuition mean it's a better school?
Pretend you're visiting three different colleges. One school gives you lunch for free. The second gives you a coupon for a discount, and the third doesn't give you anything at all. How would you react? Even if the food's not so great, free lunch is free. People like free. You'll probably like that school. If a college gives you a lunch coupon for only 10% off, you'll probably think that they're cheap and like it less. If a college doesn't give you lunch at all, it all works backward. You'll probably like that school the most; prime rib or pizza, you'll think that that lunch must be worth paying for if you have to pay for it. That goes for our perception of tuition, too. Does a higher tuition mean a better college? It might, but not necessarily.

How many colleges should I apply to?
Everyone likes to have lots of choices. Restaurants, cell phones, prom dates, all require making a final decision among many choices. If you can't decide on a restaurant, you can't go out to eat. No cell phone, no text. No prom date, no after- prom party.

You decide you want to go to a restaurant. You say, "Okay, I don't feel like Italian or Greek or diner food. I could really go for Thai or Mexican tonight." You've cut back hundreds of choices of restaurants in the Yellow Pages. Now you can narrow it down to where the Thai and Mexican restaurants are located, what they serve, which one your favorite cousin loves ("Yes!") or that cousin you hate likes ("No.")… oops, did it again. You based your selection emotionally, not logically, by considering what your cousins think. You'd do the same thing if you saw two restaurants next to each other on the street. One has a long line outside, the other a short line. You would probably go for the long line; the food must be better, right?

What does this have to do with college? The pressure to go to the "right" school can be overwhelming and comes in all shapes and sizes: group guidance meetings, hired college-consultants, prep programs for standardized testing, national magazine rankings, glossy-paper mail catalogs and appealing e-mail advertisements, everyone you've ever met telling you where you should go to college and why. Having so many choices will drive you crazy. The answer to all this stress is simple: like the restaurants, narrow down your college choices. Soon after you make your choice you'll see that choice as logical. And in a few months you'll be absolutely sure that you made the right decision after all. Good news! That school is "right" for you.

My dream school has the best program for my major. Can I improve my chance of admission?

First of all, don't commit to a major right away. Your undergraduate years are a time to explore all the interesting learning experiences college has to offer. Secondly, don't commit to the goal of being accepted to one particular school. The more effort you put into any goal, the stronger you feel about it. The stronger you feel about it, the more angry or sad you feel when you don't reach that goal. Don't put yourself in this position.

Colleges may receive 8000 applications and only have room for 350 freshmen. You should definitely apply to your dream school, but apply to others you like, too. Make a list of the schools you've chosen, ranked by preference, and keep it: it will be useful when you finally make your final college decision.

Dan Ariely, a professor and researcher of Behavioral Economics at Duke University and best-selling author of Predictably Irrational, *believes that people repeatedly and predictably make irrational decisions in many areas of their lives, including handing in homework and buying Hershey Kisses. Uri Simonsohn, a professor of Operations and Information Management at the University of California- San Diego, researched the campus/cloud phenomenon for his paper,* Weather to Go to College. *He also wrote a research paper,* Clouds Make Nerds Look Good, *about college admissions.*

(Is it predictable that professors can be fun?)

....

Sometimes we stare so long at a door that is closing,
that we see too late the one that is open.

Alexander Graham Bell (1847-1922) inventor of the telephone

....

Was the professor's advice helpful? How? Why?

Do you agree with any part of the Behavioral Economic approach?

Do you disagree with any part of the Behavioral Economic approach?

Three Student Views

You're a unique individual. But as a teenager sometimes your perspective differs from an adult's. Here's some college students' advice, based on their own find-a-college experiences.

Should I visit all the schools I'm considering?
Greg: No. One can replicate the school visit experience through the web. Some give virtual tours and have some nice maps/photos of the campus. But I definitely recommend visiting your top 1-3 schools regardless of far they may be (you're going to be traveling that far between semesters, so it's best to get a feel for it). Visits are a great time to interview, pick up more information about areas of study, and buy the souvenir college hoodie.

Make sure to visit the essentials when you visit any school. Think "where am I gonna eat/sleep/study/x?" Check out the eateries on campus. Whining aside, you're going to be eating there for at least three years of your life. Check out the dorms (the heavier the walls/doors, the better sleep you will get), and the library (how far is it from the rest of the stuff on campus? what are the hours?) You like to workout? Check out the gym. You play pool? Check out the rec area. Take in as much as possible. It will help you rest easy with your decision when the time comes.

Clare: YES. Visiting the school gives you a better idea of the people who go there, the feeling of where it is, etc. Visiting one of the colleges I thought I'd like made me realize that I didn't want to go to there. Everyone I met there was snobby and obnoxious; going to the school I attend now, everyone smiled at me walking down the street, and they were all friendly, helpful, and enthusiastic. I decided that I could live in the city after seeing it.

Charlie: I say apply to however many schools you feel like writing essays for, but don't pick a school you get accepted to without having visited first. The feel of a school is important. It may sound great on paper, but don't make the final decision without visiting. Try seeing multiple schools in the same area at the same time, but don't overdo it or the ones toward the end will seem miserable due to your fatigue and information overflow.

Should I interview?

Greg: Yes, and don't worry too much about impressing the interviewer. Obviously, be respectful; don't dress like a slob (regardless of what you might see the students wearing around campus. You get to rock the "roll out of bed 10 minutes before class" look once you enroll), and be yourself. Ask questions: any questions. The school isn't going to decline your admission just because you ask about the alcohol policy. Also, think ahead. Four years of your life is going to be awesome, but what about after that? Ask who recruits at the school; ask what alumni networks and job networks the school has. Check out career services. Nothing worse than going to a great school, making tons of friends, and graduating with honors if no companies come to recruit at your school.

Clare: I didn't do any interviews, so I don't have much of an opinion here. My guess is it depends on the person. If there's a part of your application you need to explain (bad grade somewhere, activity you want to show off your leadership role in), definitely do that, but if you're a normal student and not really persuasive, there's no point.

Charlie: If they give you a choice, why not? Most likely it will only help. If you don't interview well, opt out if you can. I don't think interviews really make any difference except for getting an alumni recommendation for some of the more competitive, elitist schools.

Does higher tuition mean it's a better school?

Greg: Yes. Like anything else, you get what you pay for. Professors are likely to be more qualified at higher priced schools (meaning they are actual doctors). Usually, more tuition dollars spent on profs, buildings, and alumni associations means better education and better support once you leave the school. Don't let high tuition scare you, either. Many expensive private schools have numerous scholarships available. There are also many intangibles about going to an expensive school vs. an inexpensive one. The amount of passive networking you're exposed to is invaluable.

Clare: It depends what you can get for the tuition. My school has an absurdly high tuition, but the housing options, social options, security procedures, and resources you have access to explain why. That shouldn't be the metric by which you judge the school, by any means, but if it's expensive, make sure you're getting a good deal out of it.

Charlie: Not at all. It just means they think they can get away with it without losing demand for admission. Lots of schools are overpriced to imply that they're better, and lots of people fall for it, assuming an extremely high price means extremely high quality.

How many schools should I apply to?

Greg: It depends. Application fees are pricy, but many public schools have network applications that allow you to apply to every school within that district with one application. I applied to one school, but was able to take advantage of a statewide college network and apply to two others as well. It never hurts.

Clare: I applied to six (four that I chose to apply to, two that my father forced me to apply to). If you're using the common application, apply to a million billion. Applying to one school I liked required several separate essays that I couldn't just have recycled, and realistically, that was my second-to-last choice. If the applications aren't much worse than the schools that you would really want to go to and especially if you can apply online, there's no harm applying to a lot of schools. But if you're not interested in the school and the application is going to take forever to do, there's no point. For example, my parents made me apply to an Honors program at a state university; the many additional essays took forever, and if I had gotten in, I would NOT have gone there because I hated the school! So it's really a judgment call, but that common application could become your best friend.

Charlie: Apply to as many as you can stand filling out applications and paying fees for. You don't need to go overboard. I did eight, and that seemed ok. Any more and I would have gone crazy. If you can creatively reuse essays on multiple apps, go for it. Definitely apply to a safety school, but make sure you'll still be happy there.

My dream school has the best program for my major. Can I improve my chance of admission?

Greg: To a point, yes. Get as much info on the school as possible, meet as many people as possible from there. Emphasize that this school is your first choice during your interview and in your essay. Sometimes, though, the school may just get too many applicants. If you still have your heart set on that school, consider going to a state school for a year and applying again. Many of the transfer students I met get great scholarship deals based on their grades from their feeder college (which were almost always higher than their HS GPAs).

Clare: I don't know the actual answer to this, but I recommend applying early decision. Not only do you prove your enthusiasm and (supposedly, anyway) improve your chances, it is the coolest thing in the world to know where you're going to school in December when none of your friends find out until April. It made Christmas the BEST, as all of my applications were submitted before Thanksgiving (Oct. 31 I got the last two finished), and my friends were still sitting around revising essays!

Charlie: Have or make connections (alumni relatives, family friends, and teachers). These days they seem like the only sure thing. A solid essay helps too. Keep your grades up and do some kind of volunteer work or extracurricular activity.

Three different college students: different personalities, different perspectives, different schools.

••

One's philosophy is not best expressed in words; it is
expressed in the choices one makes. In the long run, we shape
our lives and we shape ourselves. The process never ends until we die.
And, the choices we make are ultimately our own responsibility.

Eleanor Roosevelt (1884-1962) First Lady & civil rights advocate

••

Was any of the student advice helpful?

Do you agree with any part of the three students' approach?

Do you disagree with any part of the three students' approach?

Other people's thoughts about colleges, majors, and their careers

....

I think I approached looking at colleges backward. I assumed that I needed a goal – a major, a profession, something in mind – before I even began looking at schools. When I have children, I'm going to make sure they focus on what type of school they want and where they want to be rather than choosing a major right away. I got so nervous that I was going to be lost and unable to choose a major that I really limited my choice of schools by focusing on the majors they offered. When I ultimately decided to look based on other factors, I found what I wanted. I knew that a liberal arts background could get me anywhere I wanted to go.

Angela, Dental Student
Undergraduate Degree in Biochemistry

....

I was the first in the family to pursue a college education. I paid my own way via working, grants and scholarships. I received no guidance on career or reasons to picks a school, and school visits were done alone. The driving force was seeing my parents struggle in a failing economy. Their lack of education and formal training solidified my ideas in my early teens – I needed an education and I needed to take it seriously if I wanted to be comfortable and secure in the future.

Jeff, Director of Product/Application Development
Undergraduate Degree in Chemistry

....

I was a very talented track runner in high school and received several letters from colleges trying to recruit me. So, of course being from a family of eight and the first to go to college out of my family, I went where the scholarship was offered to pay for school. I loved every experience in college and ended up having a great track career. I talk to my son about looking at colleges not just for good athletic programs, but also academic programs. His athletic abilities may or may not pay for his schooling but, either way, his brain will outlast his athletic talents.

Saundra, Associate Director of Payroll at a major university
Undergraduate Degree in Business Administration

How has my college major influenced my current career? Let's see, Bachelor's degree in Plant Science then, 26+ years in housing finance now – doesn't seem to add up. Actually though, my degree got me the job with Farmers Home Administration because an agricultural degree was required – even though I mostly worked on housing issues. I enjoy the shocked expressions on the faces of people who ask me what my college major was when they know I've worked in housing for so many years.

Betsy, Housing Policy Specialist, Department of Housing and Urban Development
Undergraduate Degree in Plant Science

I had no clue what I wanted to major in. I ended up in my particular major quite by accident. As it turned out, it was probably something I would have chosen anyway. I deal with people in my career and my counseling skills have been very effective in dealing with "sources" and in my interrogations. Although I doubt anyone would foresee that a Rehabilitation Education major would end up as a Federal Agent.

Janice, Special Agent in government security
Undergraduate Degree in Rehabilitation Education

I felt a lot of pressure when I looked at undergraduate schools because I was salutatorian of my graduating class; my peers at school and my high school guidance counselor expected me to go to a prestigious/big name private university. As a result, I procrastinated in researching and filling out applications.

Jennifer, Medical Student
Undergraduate Degree in Biomedical Engineering

When I was looking at schools, my Dad was there for me. He knew I was debating nursing or arts. He pushed for nursing and his argument was "security and being able to find a job anywhere, no matter how big or small the city." When I made my decision to study art, he said what he thought, but was still supportive after the dust settled.

Kathleen, Photographer
Undergraduate Degree in Graphic Design and Photography

At my college, I was easily able to change my major to something that suited me better. Originally, I thought I would major in Architecture there. Soon after I got into the program I decided it would be Landscape Architecture. After the first 2 years, I decided that wasn't for me and changed my major to Urban Planning, which had been my minor.

Andrea, Civil Engineer
Undergraduate Degree in Urban Planning

My major in education did not help me immediately upon graduation, but opened doors to me when I moved into a training job at a local company and when I applied for my current job. Overall, my college experience gave me a good well- rounded education, and student teaching taught me more about myself than I had ever known before. It also made me realize what I didn't want to do.

Steve, Machinist
Undergraduate Degree in Education

Having a general business undergraduate degree makes me "qualified" for just about any entry-level position. Other than that, it's all about the life skills learned at college that help you do well at an interview and shape you into who you are when you go into the workplace.

Adam, Executive Recruiter
Undergraduate Degree in Business

When I was looking at colleges, I only looked at schools with an engineering major and made a career decision way too early. I did not have any adults who could really give me good college or career advice. If I could do it again I would probably look at liberal arts colleges. Engineering has been a great base for anything, but I was fighting my strengths, history, foreign language, and writing. I don't necessarily regret my engineering training because it has made me a great problem solver and extremely logical and analytical, and that is beneficial for any career.

Donna, Marketing Analyst
Undergraduate Degree in Engineering

Opinions & Questions...

You're attending your grandma's 80th birthday party in the local park.
A friendly cousin-in-law you've heard about, but never met, walks over to sit at your picnic table. This cousin is wearing a T- shirt with a college logo on the front. You've never heard of that school before. You decide to ask this friendly relative some questions about the school.

If you could ask three basic questions about that college, what would you ask?

If you could ask three personal opinions about the college, what would you ask?

If you could ask for three misconceptions about the college, what would you ask?

If you could ask for three of the school's strengths, what would you ask?

(What if you ended up attending a college you didn't know existed before because you talked with a cousin-in-law at a picnic in the park on a Sunday in August who was wearing a shirt with a college logo on the front?)

The Twiz Talent Show

Talented people succeed in their strengths through constant practice.
What do these talented people do for a living?

A. Sports: *What game?*
B. Musicians: *What kind?*
C. Authors: *What books?*

1) Michael Jordan, University of North Carolina: Geography

2) Dan Brown, Amherst College (MA): English & Spanish

3) Jack Johnson, University of California- Santa Barbara: Film

4) Mia Hamm, University of North Carolina- Chapel Hill: Political Science

5) Carrie Underwood, Northeastern State University (OK): Mass Communication & Journalism

6) J. K. Rowling, Exeter University (UK): French & Classic Design

7) Chris Martin, University College London (UK): Ancient World Studies

8) Tom Brady, University of Michigan: Organizational Studies

9) Stephenie Meyer, Brigham Young University (UT): English

10) Venus Williams, The Art Institute of Fort Lauderdale (FL): Fashion Design

**(Personal Space. College Major Possibilities/
Major College Possibilities.)**

Chapter 5
You-nique Essays

Apply Thyself!

··

I wasted time, and now doth time waste me.

William Shakespeare (1564-1616) playwright & poet
from Richard II

··

You barely have time for anything, with doing your homework and working after school and completing your senior project at the children's library and playing Ultimate Frisbee with your friends in the park and, of course, learning how to create a macaroni and cheese soufflé in the evening. Stop worrying, parental units. You'll get to it before the deadline. It's short. You've researched. It's…
(Cue ominous music: bum bum bummm…)

The Application.

You're smart, right? So you *do* know that if you want to go to college, completion of that college application is required, right? Websites, books, and your Guidance office contain excellent advice about completing and submitting required paperwork correctly. But for many students the most worrisome part of the application process is…
(Bum bum bummm…)

The Essay.

the (creative) *College Guide* politely offers a complementary creative perspective on writing an application essay. Even if you're not "a writer," combining your new and improved understanding of who you are as a person and as a learner, your new and improved creative thinking skills, and knowing what a school–as-a-business may be looking for, you can create a clever and unique essay.

Show the college that *you*'re clever and unique as well.

··

And by the way, everything in life is writable about if you have the outgoing guts to do it, and the imagination to improvise. The worst enemy to creativity is self-doubt.

Sylvia Plath (1932-1963) poet

··

Who wants your essay?

No Essay
Many large universities have too many applicants to review essays. Only test scores and high school grades are required for consideration.

The Common Application
You complete one Common Application and write one essay on a topic suggested on the form. This application can be sent to any of the colleges that participate in this system.

The Common Application Plus
You complete and submit the Common Application and essay. Then you complete and submit the individual school's supplemental application and required essay(s).

The Regular College Application
You complete and submit the school's own application and required essay(s).

While planning your own essay, consider who you are. You don't have to be a poet to convey an honest portrait of yourself. Reflecting your own experiences and your personality in your writing gives the reader a unique view of you. Write about what you really know and care about. An authentic admissions essay is unique, clear, and interesting. You're the kind of writer your reader would like to meet.

Here are some absolutely authentic, unedited essays written by four high school students for their college applications. All of these students were accepted into great colleges. One essay is funny, one about interests, one reflective, and one about thinking forward. You may enjoy all of these essays. You may not like any of these essays. You decide. Take out a pencil or markers and circle the good parts, cross out the bad parts. Write in the margins. Critique. Pay attention to the ideas, writing styles, and the rhythm of the words. In recognizing what you don't like in another's writing, your own writing can improve. Recognizing what you like, you'll create ideas or a style of your own.

After you've read and considered all four of the application essays, which writer would *you* like to meet?

A Funny Essay: *Chris*

In order for you to know me, you must know what I have to live with. I was diagnosed with non-nicheism[1] when I was in the seventh grade. Experts quickly realized and diagnosed my problem: I was not in a niche. My doctor told me that it was a miracle I made it through Middle School.

"Chris… you are quite the brave soul. During my research of your behavior, I have noticed that you are experimenting with several different niches: playing a host of sports, yet being in the school plays, and Boy Scouts. You see, Chris; adolescence can be a confusing time, but this is not healthy for a young man. If you continue down this path, you may find yourself having a different, and dare I say, even contrasting set of extra curricular activities. "

He began to get frustrated with my condition when I got into High School.

"Chris, I don't know how to tell you this… but your condition has worsened," he said. "These results are not good, not good at all. I see here that you insist on acting and singing in the choir, *and* playing rugby! I can't help you if you don't help yourself."

Soon, my doctor quit.
"I am not qualified to handle a case this extreme," he said.

So I was on my own. Others pretended to help, but secretly urged me to specialize; to join one niche. They didn't understand how a single person could have such uncontrollable urges to get this much out of his High School experience.

In time I learned to embrace my condition. I realized that while there were advantages to non-nicheism. I realized the diverse friends I had, and how complementary my multi-niched skills were. I realized that I could cause concussions in a rugby game, and know how to treat them from first-aid merit badge. I realized that I'm right at home thousands of feet up on a mountain skiing as well as one hundred feet below the surface of the ocean SCUBA diving. I could deliver a soliloquy just as easily as I could deliver a pizza. More importantly, I realized that committing one hundred percent to numerous activities became an integral strength.

This condition opened me up to the world of communication, or dealing with people. I learned great negotiating skills. Try telling your three-hundred-pound, tobacco-spitting rugby coach that you'll miss a tournament because it's the same weekend you have to perform in *Grease*. Or try telling your El Salvadorian-born boss who came to America in a banana truck that you can't work because you need to take the SATs. Welcome to a non-nicheisists world.

Non-nicheism has also come at a cost. I was so busy taking part in all of these extracurricular activities that school was not always my top priority, as my early GPA will show. I often missed school due to my condition: traveling to Stanford and DC with rugby, Chicago/Boston with Choir, elementary schools with plays, and Canada with Scouts. These were days out of the classroom, but tremendously educational in a different sense. The highest price of non-nicheism? While I strive for excellence, I have come to accept that there will often be niche-specialized athletes, singers or scouts who are better than I.

This condition has made me who I am. This condition has made me uncontrollably get the most out of my high school experience, but now that High School is over, where does an afflicted kid like me go?

It's like my mother told me when I was young, "Chris, hopefully one day you will find a place that is absolutely perfect for you and your condition; a place that values, even supports, your non-niche lifestyle, where people value diverse interests, a place you can call home, a place that you will love."

I can think of one.

1: (nawn · nich · izm) – An extremely rare condition found in only one homo sapien. This condition has an affect on the mind's desire to attract to one niche; this causes the human to be involved in many different, some times even contrasting, activities. See also "Christopher A."

I started writing my essay at around 3 am one weeknight when I couldn't sleep. I was really stressed out about getting into this one school, so I knew I needed to have a really good essay that would make me stand out. I didn't excel greatly in only one area, I was more spread out. I covered a wide range of skills and did them all fairly well (acting, rugby, scouts, school). The "non-nicheism" idea just came to me randomly. I thought it was a humorous way to showcase my ability to perform and hold leadership positions in various activities; all of which were unlike the others.

Your opinion?

An Interest Essay: *Kevin*

While I'm sure many have felt his influence, George Clinton of Parliament/Funkadelic has a particularly profound effect upon me. This may seem rather silly to have a man known for his funk music and wild stage shows have a serious influence upon someone, but I found that his is freedom. I've heard plenty of times what freedom is: no obligations, being simply free, free from persecution and injustice, etc. All of these are indeed free in their own right, but Clinton's music is by far more liberating, in the sense that one is free from oneself. It was odd to think about at first, but as I listened to Parliament more and more, I found that I was free from what dogged me, and everything about me was happy in the best sense. It was something akin to finally understanding Shakespeare: it was a clear feeling of "Wow." The music is both simple and complex; there is a simple melody, and beautiful subtleties. It has been said the music is the language of the soul, and I feel that this embodies that feeling perfectly.

The conductor/composer Leonard Bernstein often preached that there is no other way to accurately describe music other than to listen to it. These two sentiments justify Clinton's music in its simplest and most complex forms. Let me take an example, a more popular song by the name of "Atomic Dog." There is a very simple bass and choral figure repeating throughout, excellent for dancing, which is another basic human instinct. But throughout there is a narrator, giving the listener some good laughs, as well as providing a sort of call and response feel that derives from African music. There is also a synthesizer part that ostinates at a major sixth above the root - the note from which the rest of the music counteracts. Also, the vocals move from narrator to chorus in a somewhat fugal pattern, where the voices enter at different times, repeating a previously stated theme, which is usually modulated, but with the same rhythm.

After listening to songs like these, I feel freedom like no one could ever describe it, for what is freedom but the constraints of the mind? I feel that true geniuses in art try to mix thought with emotion, and will not separate the two, and George Clinton is no exception. While there is music that is just as enjoyable, I think anyone who wishes to truly explore music for its whole worth, Clinton should be added to his or her list. Dance, music, thought, and emotion are the keys to freedom, and if we were to lose those, that would be the ultimate demise of what we consider being free.

I wrote this essay the night that it was due and found my idea for composing it throughout the day. I got my inspiration when I was playing a Bach fugue; for some reason my mind connected the form of a fugue and "Atomic Dog." For months I did not want to write an essay about what I did, but rather about what

I believe. I wanted to show a college how I was different, and that what I was writing about was not the standard "I did this and this is how it changed me" essay. To be honest, not many people would connect the two notions I went for in my essay, and I felt some admissions officers would appreciate that. I was able to get through high school with good grades without doing much work, so I'd say to someone in a situation like mine, show a college why you are interesting and why what you have to say matters.

Your opinion?

A Reflective Essay: *Laura*

"Malika Choulette!" I shout uneasily, for the third time and, still, there is no response. Instead I am met with the usual vacant stares of twenty-something dark, sun-painted faces, that sit facing me each day, lined up outside on old rusty benches under the incessant heat of the sun, gaping at me as if I am some freak show. It must be my accent. Or maybe it's my skin. Either way it is clear that I don't belong. Tapping on the glass behind me, I tell the handyman Malika Choulette must have left. The handyman, Ansleigh Daniel, is a dark man whose thick black skin reflects the lifetime he has lived under this ceaseless St. Lucian sun. The dusty darkness of his dim complexion is heavily contrasted by the brilliant radiance of his sympathetic smile. He comes out of an office, in the same frayed and faded pink suit he wears to work every day and, facing the crowd, yells the name. Immediately, a large toothless woman rises from the benches and wobbles over. She had been waiting for over four hours to spend just five minutes with the doctor and yet she smiles warmly, handing me her number, unmistakably unaware that I had been shouting her name. It's definitely my accent. Daniel grins, shaking his head, and stumbles back to his job. I sulk in embarrassment, feeling as though I have some rare and obscene disease, as they stare at me in awe, yet, out of all of them, I am the only one who is not sick.

I have spent the past three summers in the West Indies volunteering at St. Jude, a small third world volunteer based hospital. Each summer, I lived in a sparsely furnished dormitory at the hospital, a far cry from the quintessential suburban town in which I've grown up. I initially worked at the front desk of the outpatient clinic, calling patients' names when a doctor was available and checking them in. Although challenging, after returning to the hospital for several summers, I decided I did not just want to help— I wanted to make a lasting difference.

Last year, I took action and contacted the head of the Medical Information Department who identified the need for an improved medical records management process. I eagerly accepted this project, which included identifying problems with the existing records management method, working with the staff to develop an improved method and documenting this new process. The work included sorting through over 10,000 medical files, determining their status, and organizing them accordingly; a challenging and daunting project that all previous volunteers were unable to persevere through. I constructed an electronic database to record this information (versus the manual process that was being used) as well as a back-up procedure. I instructed the medical records staff on how to use the new system, leaving them trained to carry on with this process. I issued periodic progress reports as well as a final report at the end of my stay. As a result of my work, the hospital now has a more efficient means to track patient health records, improving the level of care administered at the hospital. The staff was incredibly appreciative and presented me with a thank you note and invitation to return at any time.

My experience helping others in a third world country has affected me more than any other single experience. Living and working in an unfamiliar culture gave me a greater appreciation of diversity and a new perspective on life. The simple lifestyle and upbeat spirit of the natives that I met back dropped against the harsh realities of survival in an economically poor country made a lasting impression on me. I began to reflect on my own life and realized that it revolved far too much around material possessions. I learned to appreciate the beauty of simplicity. I learned to appreciate all that is around me, taking time to gaze at the stars and thank the wind for offering a gentle breeze. This experience taught me the value of relationships and helping others and enabled me to find myself. I am not defined by what I own, but rather by how I make a difference in the world, whether it is through my service, my knowledge or my friendship.

For my college essay, I wanted to write about something that would stand out and illustrate my character as a unique and cultured individual. After going through all the major events and experiences in my life, I decided that, above all, my volunteer experiences in St. Lucia were the most meaningful to me. After much thought, I concluded that if I wrote about an experience that had such a profound effect on my life, the passion and enthusiasm I felt would be translated to the reader, making a lasting impression. I wrote my essay just after I had volunteered, so the images were still vivid in my mind, and the emotion was still fresh, making my ideas translate easily from my mind to my paper. I wrote my essay about a month before the applications were due, and I used it for eight different applications.

Your opinion?

A Thinking Essay: *Kristen*

I am an aspiring electrical engineer, intrigued by physics electromagnetism and calculus. I have a genuine desire to help people, and volunteering at a hospital on the poor island of Saint Lucia brought me to a new realization. I saw the need for easy-to-use medical technology that is almost intuitive so it can be used by hospitals that are shorthanded or volunteer based. My goal is to combine my passions and create the needed medical technology through electrical engineering.

I have wanted to be an engineer for years and dedicated my high school career to many science and math classes in order to reach my goal. Ironically, one of my few non-science classes influenced me the most. Although this class, AP English, did not change my career choice, it changed my perspective on life, affecting everything I do. The teacher told me about a long dinner table, surrounded by great minds, all conversing with one another. Despite all of my advanced science and math classes (AP Calculus AB, AP Calculus BC, AP Physics N/M, AP Physics E/M, AP Chemistry), I still sat underneath the dinner table, hearing muffled voices of W.B. Yeats and Shakespeare. Signing up for AP English reserved a seat for me at the table and by the end of the course, I was part of the conversation.

Now I can live vicariously through literature, constantly gaining new experiences. I can examine the depth of great minds through poetry, learning what the poet questions and eventually questioning myself. With each "new" experience, each entrance into a great mind, I start to live a fuller, deeper life, instead of merely skimming the surface. Reading poems, epics, plays, and novels of great merit taught me a new way of thinking. My mind has gained another dimension: I can examine and analyze from a liberal arts perspective.

As an engineer who will create life-changing technology, it is important to approach a situation as a balanced intellect, considering both the scientific and liberal arts viewpoints. I can now pull from my library of thoughts of great minds in my head and from all of my "new" experiences. I will be an engineer who can read and write, who can communicate.

I can present my ideas and thoughts with precision, which fuels the efficient creation of well-balanced technology. I will be the multidimensional brain behind easy-to-use medical technology, and perhaps bring more engineers to the dinner table along the way.

I have been told that the most crucial part of a college application is the essay. Therefore, I started the writing process the summer before applications were due. It was stressful to determine a topic that will stand out among thousands. While brainstorming, I thought about why a college would want me in their engineering program. Engineers are usually depicted as textbook nerds with limited communication skills. Furthermore, many engineers often have a hard time relating to the average user of their technology. I realized that I defy the stereotype of a typical engineer and I wanted to accentuate this through my essay. My advice for other essay writers is to keep in mind that everyone has something unique to offer. Reflect upon yourself, extract your authenticity, and emphasize it through your essay.

Your opinion?

Laura and Kristen are sisters, writing about the same volunteer experience.
How are they alike? How are they different?

Writing Your Essay?
Think Pizza!

After a long day working in the admissions office, a tired graduate student comes back to his apartment to eat leftover pizza, watch reruns, read essays, and sort them into "No way," "Well, maybe," and "Wow!" piles on the coffee table. The higher powers in Admissions will be reviewing all of the "Well, maybe"s and the "Wow!"s next week. How can you use creative thinking so your essay lands in the "Wow!" pile?

Look at the school first. *(Explorer/ Elaboration)*
This should not be a "one size fits all" essay. Find interesting information about the school before you start. Check out the courses they offer. Visit the campus if you can. Read the school's newspaper. Explore their website. What's unique about this particular college? What do you want to tell them through your writing?

Sit down and list lots and lots and lots of ideas for your topic. *(Fluency/Explorer)*
The more ideas the better: wacky or serious or somewhere in-between. Search in different places, different times of your life, different experiences had, different toppings for your pizza. Does it have to be profound? "I really like to sleep." or "My brother secretly likes watching chick flicks on a date." might be great topics. Don't edit your brain at this point.

Play with it. *(Flexibility/ Artist)*
Think messy. Nobody's looking. Mind Map if it works for you. List if it works for you. Can you combine some of your ideas? Can you connect some of your ideas? Can you carry an idea off in another direction? What would be an interesting angle? What if...? Again, no editing at this point. This is recess.

Put it away for a few minutes, a couple of hours, or a day or two. *(Flexibility)*
Give yourself some time to let your ideas stew a bit. You may have a different perspective and some clarity when you look at your ideas again.

Read again and then decide. *(Judge)*
Which ideas work? Which ones don't? What can you change? So, what's your topic? Is it a "No way," a "Well, maybe," or a certified "Wow!"?

Write. (*Judge/ Warrior/Elaboration*)
Turn your ideas into sentences. If you don't like what you write here, move it to there. Add detail. Don't count words. This is not a final draft; it's still messy.

Use your own voice. (*Originality/ Artist*)
Read what you wrote *out loud*. If it doesn't sound like something you would say, rewrite it so it does. Admissions wants to "meet" you through your essay; they're not interested in a "blah-blah-blah," assembly-line, essay-writing, "look-what-I-wrote-aren't-I-smart?" robot. Who are you?

Relate to your reader. (*Originality/ Artist*)
Be real, even if your essay is funny. Humans share many of the same dreams, needs, experiences, and emotions. Will the reader understand and connect to the ideas you want to convey?

Watch those big words. (*Judge*)
If it's not in your vocabulary already and/or you don't know exactly what the word means, don't use it. Nobody's impressed that you can use a thesaurus.

Pull it all together. (*Judge/ Warrior*)
Now you can edit. Read the essay out loud again, double check your spelling and punctuation, cut it to the right length. (Colleges are not going to count the exact number of words. Approximate is fine.) When you're finished, send it. Now go have a pizza.

P.S. Essays are not a college admission department's evil plot to punish you. Colleges just want to know that you're a unique thinker and a good communicator.

Show them that you are.

Essay Connections...

How could you best show your personality through your writing or your topic?

How could you show your learning style through your writing or your topic?

How could you introduce yourself to Admissions through your writing or your topic?

If essays are a problem, and creativity is the solution, is the problem the solution?

Artists make their own choices from lots of other choices.

Their work reflects who they are. Can your essay do the same?

Draw a line to where they chose to go to college.

Seth MacFarlane (*Family Guy*): Animation

California Polytechnic State University

Matt Greoning (*The Simpsons*): Liberal Arts

California Institute of the Arts

Gary Larson (*The Far Side*): Communications

Evergreen State College (WA)

Weird Al Yankovic (musician): Architecture

University of Oregon

Martin Scorcese (movie director): English

University of Colorado

Vera Wang (fashion designer): Art History

Washington State University

Scott Adams (*Dilbert*): Economics

Hartwick College (NY)

Tim Burton (producer & director): Animation

Sarah Lawrence College (NY)

Matt Stone (South Park): Mathematics & Film

New York University (NYU)

Chuck Palahniuk (*Fight Club*): Journalism

Rhode Island School of Design

(Personal Space. Essay Ideas.)

(Even More Essay Ideas.)

Chapter 6
Decisions

Decisions, decisions...?

Patience and perseverance have a magical effect before
which difficulties disappear and obstacles vanish.

John Q. Adams (1735 –1826) 2nd President of the USA

In April of your senior year it arrives, announcing your acceptance to a great college. You receive more big acceptance envelopes from other great colleges over the next two weeks. RSVP by May 1st. It's time to make the decision:
Where are you going to college?

If you've loved one school from the beginning and you're accepted there, your decision is easy: you'll go there. Sometimes your decision isn't quite as easy. Your favorite school accepts you, but now you're not sure it's still your favorite. Your favorite school didn't accept you, and you have to choose between the schools that did. Your favorite school put you on their wait list, so you'll have to accept another school while you wait. How do you decide?

One of those big envelopes (or the lack of one) will change your life for the next four years. If you've already chosen your school: let the party begin! If you haven't decided what to do, this chapter will introduce you to some effective decision-making techniques. You'll also hear how real people chose their colleges. Think opportunities, question possibilities.

You're The *Judge* now: which school will happily receive your happy RSVP?

....

In many ways, picking a college is a lot like marriage:
the courtship, the ceremony, the cost. Make the
decision with both your head and your heart.

Kelli Kuehne (1977-) professional golfer

....

People spend more time deciding where to go to college for
four years than they do choosing a person to marry
and spend their life with. How stupid is that?

Larry B. (1954-) president of a successful dairy distribution business

....

Two Decidedly Summarized Versions of
Thinking About Deciding

Deciding Logically: PMI = "Plus, Minus, Interesting"
You've used this classic technique many times, and probably didn't even know it had a name.

- Take out your college evaluation sheets or Mind Maps.

- Make a three-column chart for each school. Write down the Pro's, the Con's, and the factors of each college that are different and interesting to you.

- Laying your charts out, side-by-side, compare the information and priorities you've listed for each college. What's good, what's bad, what's got what you want?

- By reviewing the data rationally, you can make a sound and sensible decision about which school to choose.

Thinking logically, which school's for you?

Deciding Intuitively: Who are you now?
You've probably changed since you began the college path. The change may be a little (you still want to be a biologist, but now you also want a campus that promotes a green, environmentally-friendly community), or a lot (you think you still want to be an engineer, but you need a college that offers other majors you might like in case you change your mind). Some colleges where you applied and been accepted may not even feel like contenders anymore. It's time to think and question.

- Recognize your personality. Will this school fit your personal goals, your priorities, or your preferred lifestyle?

- Understand your learning style. Can this college offer opportunities to strengthen your development as a learner, encourage your strongest gifts, and build all of your intelligences?

- Use creative thinking. Put aside "Who," "What," "When," and "Where." Can you look at a school as "Why" and "How?"

- Look at how the college markets itself. You were accepted, so you're in the school's target market. Is that important to you?

- You initially applied to a school because you liked it. If it doesn't feel right now, should you eliminate this college from your "possible" list?

- You initially applied to a school because it's so different. You still like it, but it means a total change in your life. Would you take that risk?

Thinking intuitively, which school's for you?

A Decidedly Summarized Version of
Edward de Bono's Six Thinking Hats

The Six Thinking Hats is a decision-making tool that asks you to look at a problem from different perspectives. Edward de Bono based this problem-solving exercise on six separate mental operations: Logic, Intuition, Negativity, Optimism, Creativity, and Organization. Your Logic provides information: "These are the positive and negative factors." Your Intuition says, "How do you feel about this?" Your Creativity delivers unusual ideas: "Can you imagine if…?" Your Organization: "We need to map out the steps to our goal." Your Optimism keeps you going: "That might be a good idea." Your Negativity can block everything: "It'll never work." If you favor only one or two of these operations, you may end up with a spiral standoff and no solution to the problem.

People working together in businesses and organizations often experience this kind of situation. Differences in personality and opinion can lead to arguments about the "right" approach to a problem, limiting a group's productivity and success. Six Thinking Hats is based on using "parallel thinking," understanding another's point of view. Parallel Thinking creates an effective process of exploring ideas, generating creative solutions, and making cooperative decisions.

To start the exercise, group members are each assigned a Hat:

White Hat (Logic): Reports the facts and data of the problem

Red Hat (Intuition): Addresses the problem intuitively and emotionally

Black Hat (Negativity): Challenges ideas that won't solve the problem

Yellow Hat (Optimism): Encourages positive solutions to the problem

Green Hat (Creativity): Explores alternative solutions to the problem

Blue Hat (Organization): Keeps the group's focus on the problem

The group goes around the table, each discussing the problem at hand only from their Hat's point of view. For example, the person with the Green Hat may only share creative ideas; the Yellow Hat points out the positive aspects of the group's ideas; the Black Hat can only look for the negatives in any solution. They then trade Hats and continue the discussion through their new Hat's perspective. Trying on different Hats, each person can reassess his or her own thoughts or positions. Generating cooperative ideas and creating unexpected solutions to seemingly unsolvable problems, the group becomes a more productive working and thinking team.

Edward de Bono has graduate degrees in medicine, law, philosophy, psychology, physiology, and design, holds professorships at four international universities, and has written 70 books that have been translated into 40 languages. Considered a worldwide expert in teaching direct thinking and structured creativity skills, de Bono believes that people of all ages should be taught to think with "simplicity and practicality." He has worked through the UN with governments to generate new ideas on international issues, provided consulting for major businesses about the necessary thinking skills in areas like management and teamwork, and created curriculum on the direct teaching of thinking in schools.

....

If you never change your mind, why have one?

Edward de Bono, psychiatrist, creativity consultant & author

....

What do The Six Thinking Hats have to do with college?

Although the Six Thinking Hats was designed for group problem solving, you can use de Bono's Hats, your creativity, and your imagination to problem-solve by yourself. So what's the problem? Deciding on a college. How can you solve it? By de-spiraling your temporarily immobile thinking operations about where to go and why. Put on a Hat.

- Get out six pieces of paper to label and write on, or cut out construction paper to make all six Hats. As you collect or remember information, ideas, or judgments about a college, you'll write, Mind Map, or draw on the appropriate Hat paper. The end objective is to see which Hat you used the most, how it relates to your own thinking, and what perspective you seem to be missing.

- Start with *White/Logic*. Write down facts you know about the college on the Hat.

- Next, the *Red/Intuitive* Hat. How do you feel about the school? What's your gut reaction about going there? Is it a school you'd enjoy?

- Continue until you reach the last Hat, then review what you've written or drawn. Like your Meyers-Briggs analysis or Multiple Intelligences assessment, you'll see that you're strong in some thinking areas and weaker in others. Try on the weaker Hats and look for new ideas and alternatives. If you find more negatives than ideas, set that *Black Hat* aside for a while you play with the other Hats.

- When you get to the point where your choice seems obvious, stop. Yes or no, you've made a decision about that college.

- Do this exercise with the rest of your college choices, compare your notes, and you'll have a winner!

The Six Thinking Hats will help you untangle your six thinking operations if approached with an open mind, and serve as a life-long skill in making sound decisons.

....

Anything that we have to learn to do,
we learn by the actual doing of it.

Aristotle (384-322 BC) philosopher

....

How did other people make their college decisions?

My parents were non-committal in pushing for one college over another, but were vocal on ones that they did not approve of. I wish that they had been more vocal on ones that they did like, because they know me so well and I was pretty overwhelmed at the time with SATs, applications, AP courses and track post-season meets. I definitely was not as open-minded as I could have been, and it would have been beneficial if my parents had pointed out how ridiculous I was being. I did not, for instance, seriously consider going to one college even though I loved the school, the students and the track coach, simply because both of my parents had gone there. I desperately wanted a place of my own. I actually applied to my college as an afterthought, mainly because it was on the Common Application and because I had loved the school's Starter jacket that I wore everyday in third grade.

Meghan, graduate student
Undergraduate Degree in English and Pre-Med

I felt pressure to go to a prestigious university, but the college I chose was the perfect school for me. It was a medium sized, Catholic, Jesuit university with a strong commitment to service and the common good. I think many adults play the "this is what I would do if I could do it again" scenario without allowing the child to choose their best fit. There is a lot of pressure in selecting a college, particularly as the cost of higher education skyrockets.

Laura, graduate student
Undergraduate Degree in Religious Studies

•••

I applied to a lot of colleges, but I didn't get into my first choice. I got into all of the other schools, so I had pare them down to choose one. I decided I wanted a school in my area of the country, in or near a city, offered scholarship money, nice campus, and positive feedback from students. When I was done sorting, I had a couple to choose from. I chose the college that gave me the most money for tuition.

Lucas, teacher
Undergraduate Degree in Education

•••

There was a strong sense at my high school that the Ivies were really the only great schools, and certain smaller private schools came in second. State schools were not that high on anyone's list – but that could be because most of the states in our part of the country don't have, or at least didn't have then, many particularly noteworthy public universities. The well-known state university I chose to attend stood out from the others. Still, when I had made my choice, I got a lot of "Oh, big football school."

Barb, Corporate Insurance and Risk Manager
Undergraduate Degree in Advertising

•••

None of my kids experienced the "heavenly choirs" thing that they say happens when you visit the "right" college. I always felt like there were so many schools out there that could be just right for them that we never even considered, because you just can't apply and visit everywhere. All of this paper that arrives, and you can't bear to throw it out, in case that school you've never heard of turns out to be The One. Now I think that kids can be happy pretty much anywhere. One of my daughters was sure she had made the wrong decision up until about November of her freshman year. And now she couldn't be happier.

Sue, Head Start Education Coordinator
Undergraduate Degree in Art Education

•••

Ask your parents, teachers, adults you like, or relatives to share their college experiences.

How did they find/apply/decide on a school?

Did they end up working in their undergraduate major?

Putting on Your Mental Brakes…

Stop! You're not done yet!
No, not this book: your brain.

Did you know that part of your brain is still developing until you're in your early twenties? Often called the "area of sober thought" or the "CEO of the brain," your prefrontal cortex is the area of the brain just behind your forehead. Neuroscience research shows that young people's brains "prune" unnecessary nerve connectors, or synapses, in their prefrontal cortex. This process eliminates neurons you grew as child and don't need now. Rewiring and refining these nerve connections helps you make more rational decisions, develop better organizational skills, and regulate your emotions. You become less impulsive and more objective.

You obviously can't make your prefrontal cortex mature faster. But when you're aware that your brain has a mind of its own right now, there are ways to compensate for your genetic and age-related lack of focus. Focus is especially important while going through your college search. Slow down, take a deep breath, and observe your impulsive and disorganized behavior objectively. Then use your creativity skills to help you identify and solve problems, get organized, and make important choices… without getting upset or stressing out. Be patient with yourself. You're just not done yet.

....

It's sort of unfair to expect teens to have adult levels of organizational skills or decision-making before their brains are finished being built.

Dr. Jay Giedd (1965-) Chief of Brain Imaging at the Child Psychiatry Branch of the National Institute of Mental Health (NIMH)

....

How might your "mental state" as a teenager effect your college decisions?

What can you do about that?

Inventors are Decidedly Amazing Creative Problem-Solvers!

The decisions of these inventors have changed our technical world.

Their college majors? It's all in the numbers...

HINT: Look at the first three answers.
Find the pattern.

A. ___ Seamus Blackley (*Xbox*): Tufts University (MA)

B. ___ Ken Kutaragi (*PlayStation*): Denki Tsushin University (Japan)

C. ___ Larry Page (*Google*): University of Michigan

D. ___ Sergey Brin (*Google*): University of Maryland

E. 1 Chad Hurley (*YouTube*): Indiana University of Pennsylvania

F. ___ Nolan Bushnell (*Atari and Pong*): University of Utah

G. 3 Jawed Karim (*YouTube*): University of Illinois

H. ___ Pierre Omidyar (*Ebay*): Tufts University (MA)

I. 2 Craig Newmark (*craigslist.com*): Case Western University (OH)

J. ___ Jerry Yang (*Yahoo!*): Stanford University (CA)

1. Fine Arts
2. Computer Science
3. Computer Science
4. Electrical Engineering
5. Electrical Engineering
6. Computer Engineering
7. Electrical Engineering
8. Computer Science
9. Physics
10. Mathematics and Computer Science

(Personal Space. Positive Direction.)

Chapter 7
Oopz.

We Awl Make Missteaks.

Never say, "oops." Always say, "Ah, interesting."

Author Unknown

You dream that you're hiking up a mountain. It's a perfect day for adventure. You've never been here before, but the path is wide and clearly marked. The sky is a glorious shade of blue. The warm sun strokes your face as you climb, and the gentle wind sends up the fragrant scent of the pines below. You finally reach the summit. You take off your boots and sit on a flat rock by a cool waterfall, happily soaking in the tremendous view from the top. (Rewind. Second scenario.)

You dream that you're hiking up a mountain. You're not sure you want to do this, but everybody says hiking is fun and the view at the top is spectacular. You decide to try it. You're nearing the top when you notice that the path is muddy and the sky looks like rain. You're sweating from the heat and humidity and all those pines are making you sneeze. Suddenly you lose your footing, trip on a stone, and fly off the side of the mountain.

Oops.

Oops happens. We all strive toward goals that we can't, won't, or don't accomplish. Sometimes you make the wrong choices. Sometimes circumstances change your plans. Sometimes you just worry about what might happen. What if you go to a college where you don't know anyone? What if you want to get away from your high school persona, but lots of kids from your school are accepted to that college, too? What if you realize your college is too competitive or not competitive enough? What if it's too close to home or too far from home? What if you want to change your major to one your school doesn't offer? What if family financial problems mean you can't afford to go to the college you wanted? What if you discover the school of your dreams is a total nightmare once you get there?

Confess: are you "What-if"ing in the middle of the night? Believe it or not, you have the power to turn "What-if"s into possibilities. Remember what you've learned about your personality, learning style, business savvy, and creative skills? Use these ideas and information, thinking, and questioning what you really like to do and what you do well.

What if that means adjusting your college choices? What if it means that you should take a break from college? What if you shouldn't go to college at all? Maybe you need to hear the advice of people who "What-if"ed about college, just like you, and lived to tell about it.

....

It is not the mountain we conquer but ourselves.

Sir Edmund Hillary (1919-2008) explorer & mountain climber, first to climb Mount Everest

....

124

One Clear Vision in the Twinge of Indecision…
Haldane's The Seven Stories

As a person with a wide variety of skills and talents, and as a future college student, you may not know what you want to do right now. What if you're good at something, but you really don't enjoy doing it? How do you find out what you want to do in life if you're not sure what will make you happy? What you learn in The Seven Stories may surprise you, or your responses might confirm what you've thought all long. Either way, it will give you the chance to examine the times you've been satisfied with your life and explore the satisfying possibilities ahead.

- Get out some paper and list twenty-five experiences in your life that made you feel good about your abilities, about your accomplishments, about others, about your world, about your childhood, about anything in your life that really matters to you. These experiences can be funny, serious, emotional, or philosophical. Take your time and write these thoughts down as they spring up. Be concrete: "Developed a six-week afternoon music program at the local senior center for my high school senior project," not "Did a senior project in music." Don't over-think or judge your answers. If you need more time, compile your list over a couple of days. Sometimes happy memories re-appear when you least expect them.

- Re-read, think, and choose the best seven of all the events, ranking them from one to seven. Write a brief paragraph for each, starting at number one and working down: Why was this experience important to you?

- Look for patterns in your answers. Are you good at being an organizer? A team leader? A creative contributor? A teacher? An environmental advocate? A performer? A hands-on worker? An event coordinator? Did you find that you like working with a team toward a collective goal, or working on a project by yourself? Did you like being in a city, a neighborhood, a rural area, another state, or a different country during these experiences? Were you happy working for an established company, a start-up business, a school, a non-profit, or as a volunteer? Were your best experiences amusing, philosophical, family-oriented, community-based, or adventurous? Look, think, and question how these experiences relate to one another.

You'll find connections between your stories that reveal who you are, appreciating your strengths, and finding out what you truly enjoy. These links can provide insight on where you should be and what you should do right now. The aim of Seven Stories is to find your passion and live it.

Bernard Haldane designed The Seven Stories technique for the business training of veterans after World War II. Haldane believed that identifying what a person does well, and enjoys doing, leads to success in their professional and private lives. He and his wife Jean founded the non-profit Dependable Strengths Articulation Program (DSAP), used worldwide, helping adults and children find their core strengths to better themselves, their work, and their community.

If you want to get the best out of a man,
you must look for the best that is in him.

Bernard Haldane (1911-2002) innovator of career development

What are my options?

If you feel unhappy and confused with this whole college-and-life mess, it's okay: take solace in knowing that other people are in the same situation.

Take a deep breath and shake off all that bad karma. Your pity party is now officially over. It's *not* okay if you sleep until 2 p.m. and have a six-month video game marathon on the basement couch (unless you're researching and designing a new game). It's *not* okay to hang out at the mall from the time it opens to the time it closes (unless you're working there to learn about retail and see how businesses work).

Doing what you like and doing it well is far better than feeling sorry for yourself.

If you want to stay in college...

Change your major.
If you're great in math but you're not happy doing math, why are you majoring in math? Math isn't your only gift. Explore all your strengths, and then decide what you'd like to study. If the new major is unusual, talk with an advisor. Most schools are surprisingly accommodating in designing an academic program that meets your needs. After all, they don't want to lose you or your money.

Transfer to another college.
You were probably accepted to more than one school. Look at those schools again. If you've totally changed your personal criteria for a college, start searching for schools that fit who you are now, and find out what transferring involves. Keep your grades up before leaving the old school: if you've done well most colleges will happily accept you.

Earn a two-year associate degree.
Many respected and well paying professions require only a two-year degree, like computer specialists, dental hygienists, registered nurses, environmental engineering technicians, radiology technologists, industrial engineering technicians, paralegals and legal assistants, occupational therapist assistants, or computer support specialists. Community colleges and many four-year colleges offer two-year programs.

If traditional academics aren't working for you...

Go to a vocational school.
These schools are two-year programs that offer degrees in hands-on professions, like culinary arts, photography, audio technology, plumbing, landscaping, advanced electronics, web development, or health care. The world needs smart and talented people in every line of work. In other areas of the world, technicians are recognized as vital contributors to their communities.

Train as an apprentice.
(No, not like Mickey in *The Sorcerer's Apprentice*.) A professional craftsman in a trade, e.g. a carpenter, an electrician, a cook, teaches an apprentice how to master the skills in their field. Usually apprentices are paid and receive benefits. Some are required to take classroom training in addition to working. Programs and opportunities for apprenticeships can be found online or even in the newspaper.

Do an internship.
An intern is a lot like an apprentice, but works for a business as a trainee or assistant. Learning how an organization runs by working with professionals gives you practical experience and helps you decide if you'd like a job in that field. Internships are temporary, offered for a designated amount of time, from a few weeks to a year, and can be paid or unpaid depending on the company. Not all businesses offer internships, but if you're willing to work for free, call and ask. You never know.

If you still not sure what you want to do...

Volunteer, in the US or abroad.
International charities, non-profits, and governmental agencies all need volunteers working for housing, family and children's healthcare, education, endangered animals, environmental issues, political issues, aid in sites of natural disasters. Choose a cause important to you and contact organizations for information. Intelligent volunteers make a difference.

Do community service.
Volunteer in your own community, at senior centers, libraries, parks, hospitals, animal rescue, schools, local political offices, food banks. You'll meet some interesting people with interesting jobs in interesting fields that may interest you.

Get a paying job in a field that's interesting to you, even if it's just for a year.

Any other ideas?

Wake up, get off the couch, exit the food court, and move on with your life.
Think, question, decide. Choose a plan that works for you.

....

Be not afraid of going slowly; be afraid only of standing still.

Chinese Proverb

....

Crash! Bang! Oopz.
People look back at their own college "mistakes."

....

The first college I attended was too small, fewer students than my high school, and the environment was depressing. Then I transferred for my girlfriend, but that second college was not right either. I didn't know what I wanted to major in and was not motivated. Then I transferred to a community college for a year, which helped me get on track and get my grades up. My last school was a good size, had a good program for my eventual major, and a nice campus environment. Looking back, I would not be in such a hurry to go to college and get my undergraduate degree. I was not ready, had NO idea about what I wanted to do and really struggled the first couple of years.

Jonathan, Retail Manager
Undergraduate Degree in Political Science

....

Any college would have been right for me. I was pretty unfocused, so my goal was to get my ticket punched with grades good enough to leave me some options. I didn't have a lot of choices at that point because (1) my high school grades were mediocre, though my SAT scores were better, (2) my parents could not afford anything other than state schools and (3) I was determined to go to a college without a foreign language requirement. (I know – slacker.)

Tim, Attorney
Undergraduate Degree in Psychology

....

I felt a lot of pressure from my parents because they wanted
me to get into the best school possible with the grades that I had
earned. I was pretty hard on myself as well. I was upset that I couldn't
really consider any of those "dream colleges" because my SAT scores
were not high enough and my GPA, although relatively high, just wasn't
good enough. Most of my friends are extremely bright, and watching
them get into good colleges I was ashamed of the schools where
I applied. I felt like I was destined for a "safety
school" or a college for average people.

Erin, Teacher
Undergraduate Degree in Education

I chose my first college because it was a two-year campus,
which forced my parents to allow me to become a non-commuter for
my last two years. Also, my boyfriend (now husband) was in school
11 hours to the west so only schools en-route were considered for
transfer. This first college was like extended high school and there
wasn't a sense of community. The second school was fine
academically, but being in the Bible belt, I experienced anti-Semitism
for the first time. I found soul mates in my Catholic
friends who also experienced prejudice there.

Bev, Teacher of the Gifted
Undergraduate Degree in Education

I wanted to be at a big school after having gone through twelve grades with the same kids, I was ready to be somewhere I could always meet someone new. My college had a lot to offer socially, athletically, fraternally, and academically. But I was pretty immature, unfocused, and an apathetic student. Perhaps going to a small school where someone noticed if I attended class, or where I actually met with an advisor at least once in four years, maybe I would have been a more serious and committed student.

Joan, Computer Consultant
Undergraduate Degree in General Science

Did my college experience prepare me for what I really want to be when I "grow up"? I'll turn 50 this year – and still haven't figured that out! There are people who know from childhood what their passion is, but I think most people spend their lives in search of the right career. And most of them settle for a job, sticking with it because it pays well, it's comfortable, or it's just too scary or hard to find their true calling.

Diane, Homemaker
Undergraduate Degree in Business Administration

. . . .

Nothing great has been and nothing great can
be accomplished without passion.

G.W.F. Hegel (1770-1831) philosopher

. . . .

. . . .

go for your passions and if you don't know what you are passionate
about then you have a wonderful adventure of listening to your
dreams - follow what excites you that you can't stop thinking about -
apprentice with people - play in the playground of life and take
time to be quiet and live with yourself - get to know
yourself - learning should be about curiosity - start
a business and fail when ever you can and get yourself lucky

Geo Geller, NYC artist

. . . .

What's *your* passion?

Oopz.

we awl make misteaks.

(But you can't make any mistakes in this twiz if you check the clues.)

A. Steven Spielberg *(movie director/producer*: Film Production & Electronic Arts) started college in 1977, left the school and returned to graduate in 2002 from…

B. George Lucas (*movie director/producer*: Film) transferred from…

C. Donald Trump (*business magnate*: Economics) transferred from …

D. Anne Hathaway (*actor*: English and Women's Studies) transferred from …

E. Forest Whitaker (*actor*: Opera & Drama) transferred from…

F. Ty Burrell (actor: Theater Arts) left college, then returned to graduate from…

G. Steve Wozniak (Apple: Electrical Engineering & Computer Sciences) left college in 1975 and returned to graduate in 1986 from…

H. Alec Baldwin (*actor*: Drama) transferred from…

I. Jerry Seinfeld (*actor*/comedian: Theater) transferred from…

J. Sandra Bullock (*actor*: Drama) left college, then returned to graduate from…

a. California State University

b. Modesto Junior College (CA) to University of Southern California

c. Fordham University (NY) to University of Pennsylvania

d. Vassar College (NY) to New York University (NYU)

e. California State Polytechnic University to University of California-Berkley

f. Southern Oregon University

g. University of California- Berkley

h. George Washington University (DC) to New York University (NYU)

i. State University of New York-Oswego (SUNY) to Queens College (NY)

j. East Carolina University (NC)

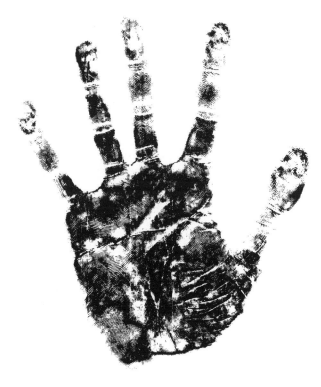

 **Thinking about Mistakes...**

....

Freedom isn't worth having if it doesn't
include the freedom to make mistakes.

Mohandas Gandhi (1869-1948) political & ideological leader of India

....

What's the worst mistake you ever made?

What's the best mistake you ever made?

Would your life change if you made a mistake about going to college?

How can you approach a mistake creatively?

(Personal Space. Mistakes as possibilities.)

con·clu·sion

1. a decision made or an opinion formed after considering the relevant facts or evidence 2. an ending that brings something to a close

the (creative) *College Guide* is about thinking and questioning during the crazy game of find/apply/decide. You've read about determining personality types (Myers-Briggs) and evaluation of learning styles (Gardner). You've looked at formal assessment of creativity (Torrance), discovering imaginative ideas through play (van Oech), and making creative visual connections (Buzan). You've learned the mental processes of decision-making (de Bono) and the stories that reveal what you want and need in your life (Haldane). You've seen what happens on the two sides of your brain (Sperry) and how a teenager's prefrontal cortex works (Giedd). You understand how college is a business, that employers are looking for creative skills, and that you're the target market for certain schools. You've listened to differing opinions about applying to schools (Adams, Ariely, Greg, Clare, and Charlie) and read real application essays (Chris, Kevin, Laura, and Kristen). You've (hopefully) enjoyed twizing the schools, majors, and careers of famous people. (Did some surprise you?) And you've heard from real people sharing their experiences and opinions about college.

How does all this relate to you, colleges, and your future?

You have a better idea of who you are, how you think, and what you want and need.

You can see increased communication and productivity in yourself by exploring your personality type and identifying your personal strengths and weaknesses. You can look for colleges that will nurture your abilities, challenge your mind, and encourage personal goals. No one thinks like you, learns like you, imagines like you, or has perspectives and passions like you. Your choices and, ultimately, your decisions should reflect who you are.

You've developed a clearer perspective of colleges' appeal and admission choices.

Colleges advertise, promote, handle public relations, sell, and market themselves because these business tools work, drawing wider recognition to a school and more applicants to choose from. Use this strategy to your advantage. Decide and apply to more than one college, just like you'd apply to more than one job. You know that acceptance is never a sure thing, but neither is rejection. You may be the type of student a college is looking for. (Or the college is not the kind of school you're looking for!)

You've learned effective creative thinking skills that you'll use for a lifetime.

You can use creative thinking skills to be fluid, flexible, original, and multifaceted in your thinking and in your actions. You can find information in novel ways and examine ideas from different perspectives. You can make connections between data and ideas. You can plan, revise, add, multiply, and revise again until you've created something unique and new. You can see patterns, purposes, and options. Remembering your past and present passions will bring positive visions of what you like to do, what you want to do, and a glimpse of where you'll be in your future.

Recognize who you are. Use your creative thinking skills. Assess the possibilities. Approach your destination with confidence. Make excellent decisions.

It's time to find/apply/decide.

Intelligence + Imagination = Success
You're smart, right?

Get out there and play!

Duh Addendum

(Extra Stuff)

....

Add legs to the snake after you have finished drawing it.

Chinese proverb

....

The Internet is more powerful than paper, especially for students, colleges, and businesses. Websites are changing all the time. Check out some of these and add some of your own.

Sites you might need for information.

College Board: www.collegeboard.com

* From the Mother of the SAT, a complete information site: testing information, advice about searching for schools, exploring schools, and financial aid.

The Common Application: www.commonapp.org

* Everything you need to know about the Common Application. Find out the participating schools and download the form at this site.

The Princeton Review: www.princetonreview.com

* SAT prep and advice about college, including majors, scholarships, and financial aid. It also links to buy their testing practice books and *The Best Colleges*, a popular fact and opinion book about 300+ schools.

U.S. News and World Report: www.usnews.com

- From the King of College Ranking, click on *Education* and find articles and information about topics like *The Best Colleges, Paying for College,* and *Careers.*

Peterson's: www.petersons.com

- Click on *Colleges and Universities* and access information about finding a school, preparation for standardized tests, and financial aid.

College View: www.collegeview.com

- Allows college searches based on area, number of students, and tuition. Other information includes advice on financial aid, application, majors and opinions of current students.

Sites you might like to explore.

Unigo: www.unigo.com

- Student opinions about lots of colleges, advice about lots of colleges, lots of video tours of lots of colleges, lots of other stuff about lots of colleges.

The New York Times' *About.com*: www.about.com

- Click on *College Admissions* and *College Life* (which includes topics like *College Football* if you're interested). Information, advice, opinions, and a comprehensive look at colleges.

- Go to *Homework/Study Tips*, choose *Classroom Performance,* scroll down to *Student Profile.* There are fun assessment quizzes on *Left Brain/Right Brain, Learning Style, College Majors*, and *Procrastination.*

Roger von Oech: www.creativethink.com

- Click on *Blog* and read creative and amusing insights and ideas by von Oech, author of *A Whack on the Side of the Head* and *A Kick in the Seat of the Pants.*

Dan Ariely, Behavioral Economist: danariely.com

- Dan Ariely, author of *Predictably Irrational*, discusses how people unconsciously make irrational decisions. Read the *Blog*, visit *Bits and Pieces* to see videos, and take tests to see if you're irrational, too.

Tony Buzan: www.thinkbuzan.com/uk

- Tony Buzan's personal website promoting Mind Mapping software. This might be an option if you like the model, but you're really uncomfortable with drawing. The site also covers research supporting the efficacy of Mind Mapping.

Edward de Bono: www.debonogroup.com

- Edward de Bono's official website. Click on *What We Do*, then *Core Programs* and you'll find information about *Six Thinking Hats* and *The Course in Creativity*.

Occupational Outlook Handbook, U.S. Department of Labor, Bureau of Labor Statistics: www.bls.gov/oco/ocos020.htm

- Describes and reviews jobs as Advertising, Marketing, Promotions, Public Relations, and Sales Managers in the United States.

The College Vocabulary

The college admissions process has its own language. Understanding the vocabulary can make the process less mysterious and more accessible to you.

Advanced Placement Test (AP) – optional tests given to high school students after they have completed certain AP or Honors courses. If you earn a score of 3, 4, or 5 (5 is the top score) many colleges give you advanced standing or course credit for that subject.

American College Test (ACT) - a standardized test that measures aptitude and skill in English, mathematics, reading and natural science. Most colleges accept ACT scores as an alternative to SAT scores on applications.

Associate Degree - a degree granted by a college or university to a person who has completed a program that requires two years of full-time study.

Bachelor's Degree - a degree granted by a college or university to a person who has completed a four-year program in science, the humanities, or related studies.

Common Application - an application form widely accepted by participating colleges and universities.

Cooperative Education (Co-op) Program - a college program integrating classroom study and work experience, offering credit and salary.

Deferred Admission– a student applies for early decision or early action and is neither accepted nor rejected by the college. The college will make their decision at the same time that they review other applicants.

Early Action - apply to a participating college or university and receive a decision from the school before the normal spring response date. You're not committed to go there and you can apply to other colleges. You're not required to make a commitment before May 1, but you are encouraged to do so as soon as you make a decision.

Early Decision – apply to one participating college or university and receive a decision before the normal spring response date. If accepted, you're committed to go to that school.

Apply Early Decision only if you're sure that you can make a well reasoned, first choice decision. Upon admission the college requires a nonrefundable deposit.

Expected Family Contribution (EFC) - the total amount the federal government expects students and their families to pay toward college costs from their income and assets.

Fee Waiver - permits eligible students to submit college applications or test registration forms without the fee. A limited number are available through guidance counselors and educational agencies for students who qualify.

Financial aid package (or award) - a combination of grants/scholarships, work-study, and loans that the college is able to offer you to meet your financial need.

Free Application for Federal Student Aid (FAFSA) - the primary form used to determine your eligibility for financial aid. Should be filled out and submitted to colleges where you applied. The deadline is January or February of your senior year.

Federal Work Study Program - an award of on-campus part-time employment for students who demonstrate financial need. The maximum amount a student can earn under this program is determined by financial need.

Grade Point Average (GPA) - a system used to evaluate academic performance. Using numerical values for grades (A=4, B=3, C=2, D=1, F=0), your GPA is calculated by multiplying the number of credits given for a course by the grade received in the course.

Grant – a financial reward based on a student's financial need, ethnicity, religious affiliation, record of achievement, association, or special interests. A grant does not have to be paid back.

Interview - a meeting with the applicant and a representative of the college. An interview allows the student to demonstrate qualities that don't show up on the school's application.

National Association of Intercollegiate Athletics (NAIA) – a governing body of approximately 500 small four-year colleges and universities for athletic recruitment and scholarships.

National Collegiate Athletic Association (NCAA) - an athletic governing body of 800 colleges and universities. Each school chooses a general division 1, 2, or 3 and is required to follow the policies regarding recruitment and scholarship awards for that division.

Open Admissions - the college admits all applicants.

Preliminary Scholastic Assessment Test (PSAT) – an abbreviated form of the SAT I, designed to give high school juniors practice taking a standardized test.

Rank in Class – a comparison of one student's academic performance with the performance of all other students at the same grade level. Some high schools do not use ranking.

Regular Decision - most colleges have an early winter application deadline of January or February. Applicants are usually notified of acceptance between March 1 and April 12. Students have until May 1 (the common reply date) to respond to the colleges.

Rolling Admission – when a school reviews applications as they are received, and offers decisions to students right away. You may apply to other colleges, and you will not be required to make a decision regarding enrolling before May 1.

Scholarship - financial assistance that doesn't require repayment, and is granted to a student who shows potential for distinction, usually in academic performance.

Scholastic Assessment Test I: Reasoning Tests (SAT I) – three standardized tests measuring students' mathematical, verbal, and writing ability and skill.

Scholastic Assessment Test II: Subject Tests (SAT II) - one hour standardized tests offered in subjects such as English foreign languages, science, history, and mathematics.

Test of English as a Foreign Language (TOEFL) - a test used to evaluate the English proficiency of students whose first language is not English.

Wait List - a school delays offering or denying admission to an applicant, with the possibility of accepting that student later. Admission of wait-listed students is determined by how many accepted students say yes to the school's offer. The college's decision process may extend into the summer. If this college is still the student's first choice, she or he must accept another school's admission and wait to hear from the first choice school.

and finally, what you've been waiting for…
The Twiz Answers!

Chapter 1: *Actors*

a) 3   b) 9   c) 10   d) 4   e) 5   f) 6   g) 2   h) 8   i) 7   j) 1

Chapter 2: *Toy Inventors*

1: Twister   2: Nerf   3: Scrabble   4: Soduku   5: Candy Land
6: Slinky   7: Cranium   8: TriBond   9: K'nex 10: Operation

Quote: "Perhaps imagination is just intelligence having fun."

Chapter 3: *Business People*

a. 9   b. 8   c. 7   d. 10   e. 4   f. 5   g. 2   h. 1   i. 3   j. 6

Chapter 4: *Talented People*

1) A: Basketball   2) C: *The Da Vinci Code*   3) B: Acoustic   4) A: Soccer
5) B: Country   6) C: *Harry Potter* series   7) B: Alternative Rock
8) A: Football   9) C: *The Twilight Saga*   10) A: Tennis

Chapter 5: *Artists*

The font of a name matches the font used for the name of their college

Chapter 6: *Techo Inventors*

Alphabetize the first names of the inventors

A) 9 B) 5 C) 6 D) 10 E) 1 F) 7 G) 3 H) 8 I) 2 J) 4

Chapter 7: *Oopz.*

A: a B: b C: c D: d E: e F: f G: g H: h I: l J: j

Sallie Ough Nangeroni

a) got a Bachelor's degree in Art Ed at Penn State.

b) taught art to high school kids.

c) got a Master's degree in teaching gifted kids at University of Delaware.

d) taught middle school & elementary school academically gifted kids.

e) had fun writing this book.

f) all of the above!

Visit
www.thecreativecollegeguide.com
for new ideas about the game of find/apply/decide!

Made in the USA
Lexington, KY
14 February 2015